LESLIE'S LEAP

Glad they managed to publish in time for your birthday —
with all our love
Nick

LESLIE'S LEAP

Nick Yapp

Illustrated by Ruby Lescott

HODDER AND STOUGHTON
LONDON SYDNEY AUCKLAND TORONTO

British Library Cataloguing in Publication Data
Yapp, Nick
 Leslie's leap.
 I. Title
 823'.914 [J]   PZ7
 ISBN 0-340-35619-7

Text copyright © 1985 Nick Yapp
Illustrations copyright © 1985 Hodder and Stoughton

First published 1985

All rights reserved. No part of this publication may be
reproduced or transmitted in any form or by any means,
electronic or mechanical, including photocopy, recording,
or any information storage and retrieval system, without
permission in writing from the publisher.

Published by Hodder and Stoughton Children's Books,
a division of Hodder and Stoughton Ltd,
Mill Road, Dunton Green, Sevenoaks, Kent TN13 2YJ

Photoset by Rowland Phototypesetting Ltd,
Bury St Edmunds, Suffolk
Printed in Great Britain by St Edmundsbury Press,
Bury St Edmunds, Suffolk

Chapter 1

The stream that ran through the Park was called a river, but it wasn't very wide. Trees, mainly willow trees, grew along its banks, and so did cow parsley, rough grass – thick in places – nettles and bindweed. On one side of the stream was open grassland, and on the other a children's playground.

It was a young stream, born only a few miles away at a place called 'Caesar's Well', and it was so shallow you could easily wade through it, but there were one or two places where it was deep enough to swim.

There was a small humpbacked bridge across the stream.

But Leslie was going to leap it. On his bicycle. Like Evil Knievel. And he was very frightened at the thought of this.

His family had lived at 143, Parkside Crescent, on the edge of the Park, for nearly a year, a quiet loop of road, in which nothing interesting happened. People washed their cars, pruned their rose bushes. The milkman drove his float. The postman delivered letters. Life tip-toed by.

When they first moved there, Mum had said:

'Perhaps you'll make lots of friends here, and you'll be able to have wonderful games in the Park.'

In the months before they moved to number 143 there had been a lot of talk about this Park. The swings, the slides, the paddling pool – which Leslie felt he was too old for – and the football pitches and the neighbouring golf course – which Leslie knew he was far too young for.

Leslie's parents were very enthusiastic. They seemed convinced all Leslie's troubles would be over the moment he set foot in the Park.

Leslie wasn't hopeful. Or impressed. For as long as he could remember, Leslie's parents had been enthusiastic.

They said things like: 'You'll love "Alice in Wonderland". It's such a lovely book.'

Leslie found it boring, and a bit stupid.

'You can have your own patch of garden and grow all the things you like best.'

It wouldn't be very easy to grow Triple Thick Milk Shakes.

No, he didn't want to go to the Oval to watch cricket, thank you very much.

Well, so what if there *was* a greenfinch swinging on the bag of nuts hung up in the tree in the garden? It would be a sight more remarkable if they'd put the nuts in the fishpond and the greenfinch had gone after them with a snorkel and a harpoon.

Stamps? Special issue stamps?

He wasn't interested.

And, most of all, where were all these friends he was supposed to have?

There was his pet – Lennie. But guinea pigs don't do a lot. You can't take them for walks, like you can dogs. And they can't learn tricks, like mice. It seemed to Leslie that all Lennie could do was go rigid with fright. It didn't seem to matter whether you approached him as a friend or an enemy. He stood stock still, with just the faintest trace of acute heart palpitation.

His family had moved so often. First it was Haywards Heath, and then Peterborough, and then Rainham, and now

Bellingham. Never long enough in one place to make friends.

Moving was disturbing. Upsetting. Waking up in a new place and finding all the rooms unfamiliar and in the wrong places. Like looking at a face and finding all the features scrambled — an ear where the nose should be, mouth on top of the eyes, that sort of thing.

And it was like weeks of camping. Surrounded by tea chests and cardboard boxes for weeks before you moved and for weeks afterwards.

'No, you can't get your toys out. They're packed now.' Mum and Dad, short tempered, rushing about.

'Where's this?'

'Where's that?'

Mum making out it was Dad's fault, and Dad making out it was someone else's fault.

And important belongings always getting lost. Lost for ever. His old comics. His collection of elastic bands. His 'useful' box of empty toilet rolls and egg cartons.

The only good part about moving was the snatched 'take-away' meals. You could count on three or four days of fish-and-chips, or Kentucky Fried Chicken, or beefburgers and fries.

You woke up in a strange room in a strange house in a strange street. Unless you could feign a stomach ache or a sore throat (and *that* was getting increasingly difficult) you were soon off to a strange school sitting in a strange classroom with strange children.

Friends.

That was the problem.

Or rather — lack of friends.

All this moving about, no wonder he couldn't make any friends.

Now that they lived in South East London, they were much nearer Nanny. Nanny was all right, but Nanny was 'family' and didn't count. Not as a friend. You couldn't muck about with Nanny.

He got used to the Southend Lane Junior School. It helped a bit, but it didn't solve the problem. Nobody bullied him. Few of them were nasty or unpleasant to him. But even when people were 'nice' it didn't mean they were friends. Far from it. Friends weren't 'nice' to you. They mucked about with you. And you mucked about with them.

But it had to be a special sort of mucking about. Not the sort Lee and Gary went in for.

Lee and Gary were in Leslie's class. They were the first children whose names he had learnt. It wasn't difficult. It seemed that most of the day his teacher, Mrs Hammond, was talking specifically to Lee and Gary. Every other remark was in their direction.

'Now, today, we're going to see our television programme — Lee, you know it's a school rule not to bring sweets to school!'

'Cough sweets, Miss. Got a cough.' Lee made a noise like a motor bike by way of proof.

'It's bubble gum!'

'*Cough* bubble gum,' said Lee, quickly, but with little hope. A phrase from a TV commercial leapt into his mind. 'Provides longer lasting relief.'

Gary's speciality was sitting in the wrong chair. This simple strategy provoked a whole series of minor, irritating rows. Gary loved them all.

Both Lee and Gary were quick to approach Leslie. They wanted to know where he lived, what football team he supported, how many times he had seen 'E.T', how far he could spit, had he ever been in bad trouble, would he like to have his ears pierced?

Boys like Gary and Lee constantly need new personnel in their lives, as familiarity breeds neglect.

They accompanied him most of the way home after school. They sent him into the Newsagents by the traffic lights to buy sweets.

'We can't come in,' said Gary, happily. 'Banned.'

One day, on the way home, they introduced him to the excitement of 'Hot Bottle'.

Leslie did find the game exciting.
He told Mum and Dad about it that evening.
'You run along the road . . .'
'The "pavement", I hope you mean.'
'. . . pavement, yeah, the pavement. And you have to throw this bottle to each other as quick as you can. Pretending it's hot, see?'
'I hope it's a plastic bottle.'
'No. Glass.'
'But supposing one of you drops it?'

Leslie didn't have to suppose. He knew what happened if you dropped it. It broke. That was the most exciting bit. Exciting and wrong. He knew that, too. Broken glass all over the road – sorry, pavement. If a toddler fell over, or a dog cut its paw, or someone got a puncture, or anything like that. A plastic bottle would be much more sensible.

He suggested this to Lee and Gary, the next day.
They looked at him in disbelief.
'Nah! What's the point?'
'Because it wouldn't break,' said Leslie.
''Xackly,' said Lee. 'So there's no point in using plastic. More point in using an old drink can. At least that makes a right old noise.'

Their other game centred around noise and annoyance. They called it Knock Down Ginger. It was a very old game, but new to Leslie.

In Knock Down Ginger, you ran along the street, ringing all the door bells or pounding on the door knockers. The essence of the game was speed, timing. You stayed just long enough to make sure you had annoyed somebody, but not long enough to get caught.

Lee and Gary persuaded Leslie that it would be a good idea to play Knock Down Ginger all the way round Parkside Crescent. Lee was caught by a sprightly pensioner, who clouted him on the side of the head. Lee didn't mind.

Leslie was caught by an earnest young man with a beard, who gave him a long lecture about caring for other people, 'you see, kid, people who, like, may be sick or, you know, kid, like really needing rest.'

Leslie minded a lot and became remorsefully tearful.

Because the game had been played in his own road, his parents got to hear of it.

There were more tears, and he was forbidden to associate with Lee and Gary.

That made sense.

So, for most of the time, Leslie made his own fun. He got used to his own company and enjoyed it as best he could. Occasionally, seeing a group of children scuffling along the road, he would feel envious. Or, watching an impromptu game in the Park, through a knothole in his fence, he would yearn to be able to join in. He grumbled aloud that it was his parents' fault, but the main reason why Leslie had no friends, as he well knew, was because he was shy. Like his parents. They were shy. They hadn't made any friends since they moved, either.

At one stage he felt so miserable he decided to leave home. And dramatically. In a way that would make everyone sit up and take notice. Everyone except Lennie.

There was a large pile of old wood at the bottom of Leslie's garden: planks, bits of boarding, tongued and grooved, old fencing posts. Leslie decided he would make a helicopter out of them, or perhaps a vertical take-off aeroplane, and leave home by flying away. No sloping off to the Bus Stop, thank you very much, only to be hauled back by Mum or Dad or a nosey neighbour. No, no, no. It would be up, up and away, leaving them all choked with sorrow and worry below.

And, once he'd taken off, he'd fly to . . .

Well, he wasn't sure where. He'd seen a programme on the telly about the Equatorial Rain Forest, and he fancied going there. He wasn't sure where it was, but it looked a lot more exciting than Bellingham. All those orang-outangs. The nearest they'd got to an orang-outang in Bellingham was the Crossing Superintendent, whom Lee and Gary swore they had seen climb up his Lollipop Stick. And, if he couldn't go as far as the Equatorial Rain Forest, there was always Hastings. He could land on the beach at Hastings. And then play on the go-carts for as long as he liked. Mum and Dad never let him play on the go-carts. They said he was too young. But *they* wouldn't be there. So he'd have as many go's as he wanted.

That had been two months ago, but he hadn't finished making the helicopter, mainly because the pieces of wood were the wrong sizes and were covered with spiders, woodlice, centipedes, earwigs and tiny red beetles.

It seemed a shame to turn what was obviously a happy home, as far as they were concerned, into a helicopter. They mightn't like the Equatorial Rain Forest. Perhaps they wouldn't even like Hastings.

Chapter 2

It was a pity. Giving up the plan to leave home. Leslie had planned to fly off on his birthday. He liked that idea. That would make everyone sorry for what they had done. He could picture Mum and Dad gazing from the dining room window as he took off. The table all laid out with a birthday tea – cake, trifle, crackers, crisps, sausages, cheese straws, the lot. And him, Leslie, outside, adjusting his goggles and taking off.

The evening after he'd given up the helicopter idea, he tried to talk with Lennie, when he took some dandelion leaves to the garden shed where the guinea pig had his hutch.

'How do other people get friends? That's what I'd like to know,' he said.

Lennie stared at him in terror, whistling slightly through his teeth, and then began to eat, also in terror.

'I mean, how do you know which people are going to be OK as friends? And where on earth do you start a friendship?'

Lennie was now eating dandelion leaves as though he'd never eaten in his life before.

'And I don't want to be friends with people unless they really want to be my friends. I don't want anybody forcing themselves. Doing me a favour.'

Lennie ate on.

'Perhaps I ought to try telling more jokes. Then people would laugh, and then they'd want to be my friend. Or do something thrilling, spectacular. It's a pity about the helicopter,' Leslie continued. 'If I'd finished it and flown away, people would have been really impressed and they'd have wanted to be my friend then.' He paused and poked the last dandelion leaf through the netting. Lennie froze, momentarily. 'Only, of course, if I'd flown away I wouldn't be here for them to be my friends.'

It was all too complicated. And depressing.

Lennie looked as though he understood that.

A week later Leslie felt much more cheerful. It was his birthday. There was cake and trifle, as he had envisaged, and there was also a bicycle. A real proper bicycle. Brand new! A Chopper! Black and silver. Very shiny. Gleaming. Leslie stroked the frame, the saddle (not just a saddle – a seat!), the wheels, the tyres, the mudguards. He sat on it, a little tentatively at first, and gripped the handlebars. He ran his fingers along the cables that led from the handlebars to the front and back brakes. He grasped the shimmering chrome bell, and then immediately set about polishing away the sticky finger marks he had left on it.

It was a beautiful bicycle.

It brought to his mind the rescue sequence in the film 'E.T.' Where the boy hero, Elliott, and his friends had used their bicycles to whisk the little creature back to the spacecraft. The thrilling chase through the town, police sirens screeching and wailing behind them, the bikes bouncing and bumping down side alleys, across the park, through building sites. And then E.T. levitating them over the police road block. Flying through the air on a bike! That must be wonderful! Much better than a helicopter.

* * *

But Leslie wasn't allowed to ride his bicycle to school let alone fly on it. The school wouldn't allow it. His parents wouldn't allow it. In the face of such dreadful ganging up on him, there was little he could do.

He had to be content with describing his bicycle to the other children at school.

'It's wonderful,' he repeated. 'It's the best bicycle in the world!' He was very proud of it.

'What sort is it?'

'A Chopper. And it's got a pump and a backrest and everything! It's just like in "E.T."!'

'E.T.?'

'That wasn't a Chopper.'

'BMX.'

The crowd gathered.

'BMX Mongoose, they had.'

'Never! Pirhana!'

Leslie tried again.

'And a real seat, you know, like a motorbike.'

It transpired that soft, padded seats, such as he had on his bike, were out of fashion. The BMX, whatever that was, had a small, hard, moulded plastic seat – functional but uncomfortable.

'Choppers are all right for kids,' sneered one Fourth Year.

'Or Grifters.'

'Yeah. But for stunts, I mean, well, for stunts – 's gotta be a BMX.'

'Like Wheelies.'

The crowd began to argue.

'What about Wheelies?'

'Mongoose is best for Wheelies. And Bunny Hops.'

'No. No. Burner.'

'All right. Come on then. You sayin' a Burner is best for Bunny Hops?'

'Might be.'

'No, come on. You sayin' a BMX Burner is best for Bunny Hops?'

Another voice: 'Course not. *Super* Burner.'
'You must be jokin''! Mongoose!'
'You don't know.'
'Come on, then. Come on then!'
The speed and intensity of the verbal conflict left Leslie quite breathless. He wasn't in this league.
'Come on then what?'
'I'm talkin' about Burners!'
'You ever done a Kiss on a Burner?'
Leslie later discovered that a 'Kiss' was when two bikes, travelling alongside each other, allowed their back wheels to touch momentarily. But that was later. For the present, he had only this vision of passion on a bicycle. It seemed highly dangerous.
'Yeah?'
'Bet you haven't. All right then – bet you haven't!'
'Shame, see, 'cos I have!'
'No – *you're* shamed!'
They were like creatures from another planet. They were more extra terrestrial than E.T. itself.
'No. You can't take it, see.'
'Right then. Right then – I done "I'm Walking Backwards for Christmas" on a BMX Pirhana, and that's God's honest truth.'
They argued and argued about the relative merits of their bikes. It seemed a fight was inevitable, until Leslie made his mistake.
The excitement had got the better of him. His mind was racing. He felt he had to say something that would cap all the boasts and challenges being flung from all sides.
'My Chopper can fly. Like in the film.'
It was like sticking a pin in a balloon. The row ceased. The crowd united to sneer at Leslie and condemn his lowly Chopper bicycle.
''E only reckons 'e can fly!'
'Leave it out.'
'You can't even do a decent Wheelie on a Chopper!'

'Have to have muscles like Giant Haystacks!'
They laughed.
'Imagine Big Daddy doin' a Bunny Hop.'
More laughter.
'Go through the pavement.'
Lots more laughter.

Leslie didn't join in. He knew so little of what they were talking about. He knew what a Wheelie was – pulling back on the handlebars so that the front wheel rose off the ground, and you cycled along, as far as you could, on just the back wheel. And he had a vague idea that a Grifter was like a bigger version of a Chopper. But he didn't know what Bunny Hops or BMXs were. And he didn't know whose Big Daddy they were talking about.

When he asked his Mum and Dad, they too laughed.

'Bunny Hop?' said Mum. 'It used to be a sort of dance – before my time. Ask Nanny, she'll know.'

By the time he next saw Nanny, Leslie had forgotten what question he had asked Mum.

'Nanny, what's a BMX?'

His Nanny gazed thoughtfully at the television set before answering. She spent a lot of time gazing at the television set, especially when it was switched on.

'Beemax,' she said. 'You don't often hear about that nowadays. Haven't seen it for years. Used to get it at the Chemists. What were they called? Prossers? Proctors, that's right. Proctors the Chemists. Didn't like it much. Got no taste. But our Aunt Lou swore by it.'

Nanny turned her attention back to the television set. Leslie looked at her, a little in awe. He had this mental picture of his Nanny, first licking and then biting and eating bicycles. No wonder she had trouble with her teeth. He wondered how much of the bicycle she used to eat. All of it? Mudguards, tyres, chain and all? Or just the frame? And what about the spokes? A bit like sword swallowing, he reckoned that would be. And the inner tubes would give you dreadful wind.

When Nanny had gone home, he mentioned the subject to Mum and Dad.

'I wish I'd known Nanny when she used to eat bicycles.'

His parents looked at each other.

'It's because he's an only child,' Mum said. 'And having no friends.'

'She's *your* mother,' Dad said. 'There's no knowing what nonsense she tells him.'

'And you can't get bicycles at a chemists now, can you?' said Leslie.

Chapter 3

Leslie's teacher, Mrs Hammond, was older than his Mum, younger than his Nan, Leslie thought, and she was kind and cheerful and spent most of her day sitting down.

Some of the other teachers, the younger ones, spent most of the day standing up and moving about very briskly, as though it was harder to hit a moving target. Leslie preferred his teacher to stay in one place. So that he knew where he could find her.

Mrs Hammond was very thorough and careful and painstaking in her teaching. She was well organised. She knew what she wanted from each of the children in her class. Most of them liked that. They enjoyed the regular spelling tests, and reading sessions, and story times, and the next piece of Maths always being ready for them the moment they finished each workcard. They were also grateful for Mrs Hammond's rugged good health. She was never absent.

Only Gary, Lee and one or two of their mates weren't appreciative. Lee found schoolwork difficult. The way his books kept leaping off the table on to the floor. The way his pencil point, whenever faced with a spelling test, committed suicide. The way his Arithmetic Tables Chart was different from everyone else's.

'Eight fives,' said Mrs Hammond.

'Forty,' said Leslie.

'Good. Lee – six threes.'

'Sixty three,' said Lee, without a second's pause.

'Wrong. That's a silly answer.'

'Yer, Miss,' said Lee, who had expected it would be.

'Gary?'

'All right, Miss?' Gary was always asking people if they were 'all right?' It was a habit he had picked up from his mother. He believed it made him sound very caring. Mrs Hammond found it intensely irritating.

'What's the answer?'

Gary had been playing, under the table, with a hand-held video game – a very small one. He not only didn't know the answer to Mrs Hammond's question, he didn't know the question itself, or the lesson, or the day of the week. He was at a disadvantage.

But, on the whole, Mrs Hammond got on well with her class. They liked her methods, they liked her ideas, and they liked her.

She made them do what she called 'Research'. She had long ago discovered that the words 'Topic' and 'Project' carried no weight at all with the children. Nor with their parents. 'Research' on the other hand, sounded very grown-up. It was what governments and laboratories did. There were programmes about 'Research' on the telly. There weren't programmes about 'Topics' or 'Projects'. And the adults were very pleased – 'that Mrs Hammond's got our Linda doing Research. Shows she must think well of her'.

Early in the summer term, Mrs Hammond told Leslie and three other children that she wanted them to do some research into Pets.

'First find out what pets the children in our class have,' she said.

They discovered that the twenty-eight children in the class had, between them: five dogs, six cats, four rabbits, three tortoises, one hamster, twenty-nine gerbils ('But my Dad's making me get rid of a lot of them,' said their desperate owner), two mice, one budgie, a 'used-to-have-a-parrot', and Leslie's guinea pig.

'Then find out all you can about what sort of hutch or kennel or cage they should have, and what they should eat, and anything else that's important.'

One of the things Leslie discovered in his research was that guinea pigs need a companion. A hutch mate. A friend!

He told Mum and Dad, at tea, in the hope that towards the end of the day, when work was done and they were relaxing, would be better.

'Listen – "A guinea pig should not live on its own. It needs a companion".' Leslie looked up from the book he was reading. 'I think Lennie would like a dog as a companion.' He talked quickly, hoping to overwhelm Mum and Dad with the speed of his suggestions. 'A dog would be good. It would be someone for Lennie to talk to. He could take it for walks. In the Park. It would protect him. Then you wouldn't need to be worried about him being picked on by older boys.'

'Older *boys*?' said his Mum. 'Don't you mean older guinea pigs?'

'Them too,' said Leslie, working hard to establish an atmosphere of agreement and co-operation. 'And there wouldn't be any eating problem, because dogs eat meat, being carnivals, and guinea pigs eat pellets, being . . .' Leslie paused, unsure of the word.

'Herbaceous?'

'Yes, Mum, that's it. So they wouldn't eat each other's food.'

'Isn't there a risk that a dog would eat Lennie?'

Typical of Dad to be pessimistic, thought Leslie, and when a dog would be such fun, too.

'I don't think a big dog would eat Lennie.' Leslie liked the idea of a really huge dog.

'Why not?'

'If it was a big enough dog, it sort of wouldn't notice Lennie. Its head would be too far from the ground. And it would be a much better friend for me . . . for *Lennie*, I mean.'

'We are *not* buying a dog. You can't have a decent garden and keep a dog.'

'And I don't want the sofa and the carpets covered in dog's hairs.' It was Mum putting an end to the discussion by beginning to clear the table.

Leslie hadn't held out a lot of hope for a dog. His reasonable alternative was ready.

'All right, not a dog, a monkey.'

He could see from their faces and the way Mum stopped in the doorway, that they didn't think a monkey was a reasonable alternative.

'Parrot?'

'Pony?'

'Some rats?'

Leslie felt bitter, and made the mistake of trying heavy sarcasm.

'Perhaps,' he said, his mouth in something of a sneer, 'perhaps it wouldn't be too much trouble if I could have a small bucket of maggots. Or maybe just one maggot. Since you don't seem to want me to have a proper pet.'

His heavy sarcasm brought its usual wrathful response from Mum and Dad.

There was a scene.

They seemed to be against everything. You could get diseases from parrots. It was cruel to keep birds in cages. A pony was too expensive. There was nowhere to keep a goat. Neither of them could stand snakes. His Mum hated rats.

Then the discussion broadened. Mum and Dad recited a catalogue of every single little tiny mistake he'd made in the whole of his life. He never fed Lennie without someone reminding him. He couldn't keep his own room tidy. What about those nails he bent with his mad helicopter scheme? The windows he broke – they made it sound like one a day. That trouble with Gary and Lee and Knock Down Ginger. On and on and on they went.

There were tears from Leslie, and Dad had to have a drink. In the end they said he could have a tortoise.

Chapter 4

So Leslie bought a tortoise, which he called Luke Skywalker, in the hope that it would make him feel better about its being only a tortoise.

It didn't.

Luke was brought home in a cardboard box from the Pet Shop at Downham, and introduced to Lennie. It was not a very promising meeting. Leslie didn't see how a tortoise could possibly inspire such fear, but Lennie presumably had his reasons.

Over the next couple of weeks Leslie watched his two pets closely. Would they become friends? And, if so, how? How could you tell when a guinea pig and a tortoise became friends? Would they mate, and produce a Torty Pig or a Guineaoise? Presumably, if they did, the cowardice of the guinea pig and the shyness of the tortoise would combine to produce a creature that *never* came out of its shell.

But Lennie and Luke Skywalker showed few signs of friendship. Occasionally they trod on each other, but that was about it.

Leslie early abandoned the idea of taking his pets to the Park. They wouldn't enjoy it, and they would be poor, not to say, slow company.

Now that he was nine, however, Leslie decided it was time to step up his campaign for greater independence, the main object of which was to persuade Mum and Dad to let him cycle to the Park on his own.

He went into action one Sunday, when Nanny was on a visit. He hoped to get support from her.

'I'd be really careful,' said Leslie.

'What are you talking about?' said Mum.

'The Park. If I went on my bicycle to the Park. I'd be really careful. I wouldn't have anything to do with strangers. I know all about that. We had a policewoman come to school. She told us the Four Don'ts – Don't talk to strangers. Don't go with strangers – like if they ask you to get in their cars. Don't take sweets from strangers.'

He paused.

'That's three,' said Dad. 'What's the other one?'

'When I was a girl,' Nanny said, 'we didn't have strangers. Everyone knew everyone.'

Leslie racked his brains for the fourth Don't.

'You could get a 56 Bus from Tottenham Hale, to go down the Docks, and go upstairs, and not a person there but you didn't know.'

It was untrue, but Nanny like to make her contribution.

'When you were a girl, when you were nine, were you allowed to go to the Park by yourself?' Leslie looked to his Nanny for a helpful, supportive answer.

'Course I was!'

'There!' Leslie turned in triumph to Mum and Dad.

'But there wasn't the mugging there is now,' Nanny added, with relish.

Leslie sighed. So helpful!

'I've remembered the fourth Don't,' he said. It wasn't true, but he had at last invented one that sounded right. 'It's Don't buy a secondhand car from a stranger.'

'Rubbish,' said Dad. 'It's Don't buy a secondhand car from a friend.'

Mum looked at both of them. 'I sometimes wonder about both of you,' she said. 'Have you ever heard of anyone trying to sell second-hand cars to children, in the Park?'

'I wasn't talking about the Park. Or about children,' said Dad, testily. 'I was merely pointing out that it is a sound general principle not to buy a secondhand car from a friend.'

It had all the makings of one of Mum and Dad's really heavy conversations.

Leslie intervened.

'Please may I cycle to the Park by myself?'

'What do you think?' Mum was asking Dad.

'He'll be all right so long as he chooses his companions carefully.'

Leslie's dramatic side took over.

'Have I ever, *ever*, had the wrong companions?' Such unjust accusations!

'There were Lee and Gary. Gary and Lee are what I call "rough" children.'

'OK, OK,' said Leslie. 'I won't play with any rough children. Only smooth ones, I promise.'

'Is that supposed to be clever or rude?' Mum asked.

'No. Neither.' Leslie's aggrieved innocence increased.

Nanny started to laugh.

'Smooth children,' she said. She shook a little, and rocked to and fro. Then she knocked her side plate off the table.

Tension mounted. Dad stopped carving the meat and shot a quick look at Mum. He made his breath hiss slightly through his teeth.

'Ooo-er,' said Nanny. 'Still, no harm done.' She stooped, to pick up the plate with her left hand, and managed to stick her right hand in the butter dish.

Leslie smiled at her. It was interesting, what she was doing. Then he looked at Mum and Dad and his smile disappeared. It was going to be one of *those* meals.

'I'm not being rude or clever. I wouldn't ever be rude. Especially not in the Park. And – and . . .'

Inspiration came.

'And I'd always come home at the right time.'

They made him promise. All those things.

And all those things Leslie managed with no difficulty. He wasn't sure what distinguished 'rough' children from 'smooth', but he wasn't much bothered by either.

He was far too busy watching the antics of the groups of children who spent all day cycling up and down, across the bridge, over the stream, round and round the playground. Shouting at each other, ringing bells, sounding horns, sirens, always making a lot of noise. Sometimes they got off their bikes, and the boys among them had a mud slinging fight across the stream, flinging clods of earth and small stones, and still shouting and making even more noise.

Leslie was irresistibly drawn towards watching their cycling. For they were superstars of the bicycle.

On the playground side of the stream the ground was several feet higher than on the playing field side. A steep slope ran down to the stream, through a small clump of willow and hawthorn trees. The grass was worn away, and a few straggling roots jutted through the light brown earth, which had been packed hard by the passage of the bicycles, up and down, up and down.

There, on their bicycles, the children 'showed off', zigzagging through the trees, throwing in the occasional Bunny Hop, jerking the front wheel off the ground and then bumping the back wheel along. Or cycling flat out across the grass at the top of the slope. Or starting up and going straight into a Wheelie, pulling effortlessly back on the handlebars, pushing their weight into the back of the saddle, raising the front wheel above their heads, and pedalling, not once or twice, but ten, fifteen, even twenty times before bringing their front wheel down again.

Sometimes they placed one bike upside-down on the grass and performed what seemed to Leslie their most dangerous feat. They cycled straight at the upside-down bike, as though going to ram it, and then, at the last moment, when Leslie felt his stomach do a flip-flap, they leapt into the air, on their bikes, and passed between the front and back wheels of the upside-down bike, landing, with a bump and a roar of bravado, a few feet the other side.

Or they cycled at breakneck speed down the slope, at the stream. By jamming on the back brake and twisting the handlebars, they swerved the bike round, inches from disaster, and set off back up the slope. Mud flew as the tyres scratched at the ground, and there was a slight hiss as the pellets of hard earth and the small stones, torn from the ground, skimmed into the stream. Once at the top of the slope, they pulled on the handlebars, and, gripping the frame of the bike between their knees like an expert horse rider, slewed their bodies round so that the bikes spun like coins, like ice-skaters, to face back the way they had come. And so, off again.

It wasn't merely exciting. It was breathtaking. If they seemed to have the dexterity and manoeuvrability of a skater, they had the power of a motor cyclist. Their bikes had bright plastic wheels, fat tyres, chrome badges, and thin silver masts with pennants flying from them. They were like knights of old. And they cycled singly, in pairs, and sometimes in thrilling formations. The riders wore shiny shorts and 'flash' T-shirts. Some had red caps with long, stiff peaks. Some had safety helmets. Some had elbow and knee pads. They all wore trainers on their feet.

They were good, and they knew it.

Leslie wanted to be like them, to be one of them, more than anything else in the world.

The beauty, the glamour of it all was too much. He had to try.

It meant waiting until the Park was almost empty, certainly until 'they' had all gone, cycling off with the same whoop and holler that they made on arrival and while performing their stunts. Leaving behind them a little settling dust, and a tear-stained vision, as though the Circus had packed up and moved off to another town.

Leslie stayed on, hiding himself and his bicycle behind an elder bush. Once all was quiet, he wheeled his Chopper out, over the bridge and towards the clump of trees.

He sat on his bicycle at the top of the slope. It was like staring from a cliff top, over a precipice, down to the roaring sea below. But he had to find out. He had to know what it felt like, to let go. To put your trust in your skill and your machine, in your brakes and your legs and your instincts. To dare to 'show off'. What was it the wizard said in 'Star Wars'? 'May the Force be with you'? No, '*trust* the Force', that was it. Let all doubts and worries go, and feel free.

It was frightening. Frightening? It was *terrifying*! He had no idea what would happen, but he had to find out if he was any good or not.

So he pushed off with his left foot, and pedalled with his right, plunging down the slope.

What happened after the first two 'pedals' was fearful. Like Lennie, Leslie gave up. There was nothing he could do. His muscles locked. His brain refused to make any useful suggestions. He was stiff with fear as the bicycle bucketed down the slope to the stream. Leslie couldn't apply the brakes, he couldn't turn the handlebars. He couldn't yell or scream, leap off or fall off. For one stupid second he thought: 'This is how a guinea pig feels.'

Like a toy, plastic motorcyclist on a toy, plastic motorbike, he could only go where his machine went.

And off the bank and into the stream he and his machine went, clattering over a spit of gravel, and plunging into deeper water beyond. There he fell over, his hands still clamped on to the handlebars, and his legs still gripping the frame.

The water was cold, and deep enough to remind him that the stream was called a 'river'. Fortunately, the bottom here was mud and shingle, with, apparently, no broken glass.

He got up. His bicycle was a little scratched, but no great harm had been done to it. He was bruised and soaked, but no bones were broken. It could have been worse.

He lugged his bicycle out of the stream, and walked it home.

Mum and Dad were furious. He was late. He was wet. He was hurt. Three good reasons, they seemed to think, for being cross with him. Their anger matched his own. All three of them – Mum, Dad, and Leslie – were cross with Leslie.

He went to bed and cried.

Chapter 5

His bruises healed, his cuts healed, Mum and Dad's tempers healed. The lasting results of his reckless attempt were a few ugly scratches on the forks and mudguards of his bicycle, and a change in his attitude to Lennie.

It was awful to be a guinea pig! Awful! To feel like that!

'Something's got to be done about all this, Lennie,' he said. 'I don't like being a guinea pig, and neither do you. The only difference is, you've got to be one, and I haven't.'

The problem was 'how to change'. You didn't wake up one morning and find you weren't a guinea pig. Nor did it seem merely a question of making up your mind to change. You didn't become older, better, tougher, wiser, cleverer – just by deciding you wanted to be all these things. It was like the problem of friends. He *wanted* to make friends, to have friends, to *be* friends, but that hadn't so far made anything happen.

Leslie went on being angry with himself for days – long after Mum and Dad had forgotten all about it. Then his anger turned to despair.

He discussed the problem over the phone, with Nanny.

He was allowed to phone Nanny. It was only a local call and it kept both Nanny and Leslie occupied. 'Keeping Nanny and Leslie occupied' was one of Mum and Dad's major concerns.

'Hallo, Nanny?'

'Who's that?'

'Me. Leslie.'

'Hallo, Leslie dear. How's the world going? Round?' Nanny always said that.

'What's the worst thing that's ever happened to you?' said Leslie, who liked to be direct on the phone.

'Ooo-er,' said Nanny. 'The worst thing? I lost me teeth once. On a bus. A 65 bus, I think it was.'

'Did you want to kill yourself?'

'It must have been a 63. Now where was I going?'

'What did you do when you lost your teeth?'

'I can't remember, dear. Must have borrowed someone else's. Can't have mattered that much, but I know I was very upset at the time.'

'Did you ever crash into a raging torrent on your bicycle?'

'Not many of us had bicycles. We used to make our own fun. Your Great Uncle Bertie had a concertina, and we used to sing. Or make up plays. Or play "Posh Lady".'

'How do you play that?'

'One of us would pretend to be the Posh Lady and would walk up and down, and the rest of us would jeer and spit at her. It was a horrible game. But then we all hated having to make our own fun.'

'The point is, Nanny, what am I going to do about it?'

'About what, dear?'

Did she *ever* listen.

'About cycling into a raging torrent!'

'I should try to avoid them, dear. Take no notice of them. Maybe they'll go away.'

You couldn't rely on Nanny to be helpful. Leslie put the receiver back on its rest.

* * *

So, how was he to become older, tougher, wiser, cleverer?

He considered them in order.

Getting older. Well, that wasn't difficult. Happened every day. But not fast enough. Leslie wondered if there was a way to speed up the ageing process. He remembered how often his Mum told him, nagged him, that reading in bed too late at night would give him dark rings round his eyes. Most old people he knew had dark rings round their eyes. Dark rings all over their faces.

What was the other thing? Frowning. Whenever he frowned, Nanny said: 'The wind'll change and you'll be stuck like it.'

Leslie frowned through the window at the trees in the Park.

It was a warm, still, June day. There was no wind.

Leslie's frown deepened.

It was going to be a job, getting older. After five minutes frowning, he had a slight headache and found it hard to focus his eyes.

Tougher? Wiser? Cleverer?

School was supposed to take care of 'wiser' and 'cleverer'. What about tougher?

That was largely a matter of acting 'tough'. Like Lee and others did in the playground. Going up to people, shoving them in the chest, thrusting the jaw forward, breathing hard, flaring the nostril, threatening.

Leslie practised all this at home, in front of the hall mirror. He was impressed. It certainly looked tough.

Next morning, Leslie strolled into the playground. He gazed round, looking for an opponent.

Lee. Why not Lee? Start at the top.

Leslie sauntered up to Lee.

Lee smiled at him. ''Allo, Leslie,' he said. 'All forgiven, is it?'

Without warning, without cause, Leslie shoved Lee in the chest, and attempted to snort and flare his nostril.

The attempt brought on a coughing fit, and, at the same moment, Lee pushed him in the chest.

'Who d'you think you're pushin'?' said Lee, pushing him again.

Leslie stumbled backwards and tripped over.

'You're 'ard, aintcha,' said Lee with a sneer.

Lee moved away, and Leslie slowly picked himself up.

Wonderful, that had been!

Really tough!

He looked across the playground.

In a corner, near the drinking fountain, were a couple of First Years. Small, harmless, vulnerable – shy! Very like the Leslie of former days. That was more like it.

He went over.

'Hey – you!' said Leslie.

The two First Years looked up at him.

'You want bother?' said Leslie.

'No.'

'Know who I am?'

'No.'

'I'm Mr . . . er . . . Mr . . .'

He couldn't remember. What was it? Mr Large? Huge?

'I'm Mr Biggs.' That was it.

The First Years stared at him, not sure what to do.

'Just you remember that. See?' Leslie pushed the smaller of the two on the shoulder.

'Leslie!' Mrs Hammond's voice cut through the babble of the playground. 'Leslie! How dare you! Outright bullying. I'd never have expected it of *you*! Go and sit in the classroom for the rest of playtime.'

The older, wiser, tougher, cleverer Leslie walked swiftly and stiffly back across the playground, disgrace dripping off him.

As he left, he passed Gary.

'All right, Leslie?'

Huh!

And then, for the first time, Leslie met the Gang.

One hot afternoon, after school he was cycling slowly to and fro, in the Park, deliberately keeping away from the stream, when he saw them.

A Gang. That was the only word for them. The way they were laughing, shouting, jostling and bumping into each other. A Gang of Rough Boys. No, on closer inspection, a Gang of Rough Boys and Rough Girls.

There were eight of them. Eight children and two skateboards and one length of rope.

Two of the boys were sitting on the skateboards, leaning backwards and sticking their legs straight out in front, and holding on to the two ends of the rope. The other six, three boys and three girls, were all pulling on the rope and dragging the skateboarders along. Bumping noisily and uncomfortably over the playing fields. Laughing — a great haze of laughter hung over the group. Occasionally one of the skateboarders would fall off and sit heavily on the ground. There would be more laughter and delighted yells.

'Whoa up! Old Mark's off again!'

'Banged his bum good and 'ard.'

'Don't pull so 'ard on the bloomin' rope.'

'Tell you what, let's run. Let's see what 'appens when we run.'

'Don't you dare.'

'Come on, Tricia. Run. Pull, pull!'

'Slow down. Flippin' nut cases, all of you.'

''Ere, 'old it — I reckon I'm gonna be sick!'

'Ergh! Dirty Devil!'

'It's too 'ot, let's 'ave a breather.'

They stopped, only a few metres from Leslie. He was leaning on his bicycle, staring at them.

One of the girls said: 'That kid over there thinks we're all nut cases.' She called out to Leslie. 'Don't you?'

There it was again. The Guinea Pig Feeling. Don't say anything. Don't do anything. Stand stock still and maybe it will go away. Whatever it is.

No, no, no, thought Leslie. I *won't* be a guinea pig.

He cleared his throat.

'No, I don't,' he said.
'Whatcha staring at then?'
'Er...'
'Do you want a go?'

It was one of the boys asking. Asking him, Leslie, if he wanted a go.

'No, thank you very much all the same. No.' Leslie could have kicked himself. Might as well go and find some dandelion leaves to chew. It was all he was fit for.

'Come on! Have a go!'

The boy was holding the skateboard towards him.

''E can't be worse than Derek,' said another girl.

It was obvious, from what happened next, which of the boys was Derek. The girl was pushed to the ground. Derek's victory was short-lived, for she grabbed his ankle and twisted it.

'Aaarrggh!'

It was an exaggerated cry of pain – a clear bit of acting, of pretend. But Derek fell to the ground beside the girl. She had torn up two fistfuls of grass which she good naturedly threw in his face.

'Aaarrggh!' screamed Derek. 'I'll never walk again!'

The skateboard was still being offered to Leslie.

'Go on,' something inside him said. 'Go on. Now. Or never.'

He let his bicycle rest on the grass, and walked over and took hold of the skateboard.

'Ever done any before?'

'No.'

''Ere, can I 'ave a go on your bike?'

'Don't let 'im – 'E'll most likely break it.'

'Jus' by lookin' at it.'

More laughter and more pushing and more wrestling.

Leslie heard himself say; 'Yes, you can borrow my bicycle.'

His voice sounded different from theirs, and they noticed.

'Oh, thanks most awfully. I'll take jolly good care of the bicycle, old fruit, don't you know.' It was not an impersonation, but a piece of ridiculous exaggeration – clearly Derek's trademark.

'Take no notice of 'im,' said the girl who had twisted Derek's ankle. ''E's only allowed out of the loony bin for an hour or two Thursdays. We've promised to get 'im back there for supper.'

Derek was already cycling madly up and down, making a noise like a police siren. The rest were lolling on the grass. Now and then they looked at Leslie. Friendly looks.

They were all older than him, Leslie thought. Perhaps only by a year or two in some cases, but it seemed more. They were definitely the sort of children that he reckoned Mum and Dad would call 'rough'. You couldn't tell by their clothes – they were mostly wearing T-shirts and jeans or cords, one of the boys was stripped to the waist. It was something in their manner. And little things. Details. One of the boys had a stud in his ear. Another was a real skinhead, with boots. One of the girls was wearing what looked like a man's hat.

But in other ways they didn't look very different from him. A couple had scooby-do's hanging from their waistbands, the same as him. And one had an Arsenal T-shirt, and Leslie supported Arsenal. He'd never been to see them play, and he had no idea who was in their team, but he supported them. You had to support someone, didn't you?

'Well, go on, then.' The big boy who'd offered the skateboard was smiling at him. 'Sit on it and we'll give you a ride.'

'No, we won't. We're 'avin' a rest.'

'I'll pull you.' It was the boy who'd been having a ride when Leslie first saw the Gang. What was his name? Mark?

'Thank you, Mark,' said Leslie, politely.

''Ow d'you know my name's Mark?'

'I heard the others call you that.'

One of the girls called out: ''E ain't like the rest of you. 'E's got brains. You know – up 'ere.' And she tapped the side of her head.

As she did so, the boy next to her made popping sounds like corks being pulled from bottles. It made it sound as though her head was empty – echoing.

Leslie and the others all laughed.

He felt better. Sufficiently so to sit on the skateboard and take hold of the rope.

They pulled him, the big boy and Mark. They pulled him slowly and gently at first, and then faster, sometimes changing the angle of their pull, so that the skateboard curved out in a wide arc, gathering speed, and usually shooting Leslie on to the grass.

He fell off dozens of times. He'd no idea how many. But he got very excited and laughed and laughed and kept getting back on.

It was wonderful.

When he leant back, it was as if the grass was zooming over his head. He imagined he was a jet-propelled fieldmouse. He wondered if insects would be sucked up his nose. He gazed up at the blue, cloudless sky, giggling and giddy. Once or twice, when he fell off, he rolled over and over.

They asked him his name, and immediately shortened it to 'Les'.

'Come on, Les. Up you get.'

'Derek! Come over 'ere with Les's bike!'

Most of them had a go on Les's bike. Some did tricks, standing on the seat, riding facing backwards, or resting their feet on the handlebars. Derek's speciality was cycling up and down, flat out, screeching out a running commentary on what he was doing.

'. . . and now he's goin' faster than the speed of sound . . .'

'Wish he was,' muttered one of the girls.

'. . . and now faster than the speed of light . . . and now faster than the speed of dark! And he's into orbit . . . he's broken through the gravity shield (he'll mend it on his way back) . . . he's cycling round Mars . . . he's cycling round Crunchie . . . he's . . .'

There was a clattering noise, and a few bumps. Derek had fallen off, not for the first time.

'Gone down a Black Hole,' said Mark.

'Good riddance.'

In the beginning Leslie was worried about what might happen to his bicycle. As he became more excited he stopped worrying. He was enjoying himself.

He learnt their names. The big white boy was called Steve. He wasn't the leader – the Gang didn't seem to have a leader, but Leslie noticed Steve was often the one who directed the Gang, made suggestions as to what they should do next. The two black boys were Mark and Wayne. Then there were Derek and Tricia (white), whom he now recognised easily – and the two other girls, Sharon (black) and Margaret (white). Margaret was sometimes 'Maggie', but more often 'Tilt', a nickname given her because she leaned slightly to one side when she was standing still. Lastly, there was a boy whom Leslie thought of as being 'a bit overweight'. He was, in fact, a fat boy, whose name was Philip, but who insisted that he was 'The Great Dalrymple'.

They were fun. They were more than a bit nuts. The Great Dalrymple spent much of the time trying to skateboard on his head.

Derek, who had fallen off Leslie's bike into a patch of nettles, was staggering about the Park.

'Will the daring explorer find the antidote for the appallin' snake venom with what his veins is stuffed? The sun beat mercilessly down. 'E could 'ardly drag 'is pain racked body through the jungle.' Looking up and seeing that only Leslie was paying him the slightest attention, Derek's voice changed. 'Anyone got enough money for a can of Coke?'

They took no notice.

'Or a packet of crisps?'

The girls were dancing. Wayne and Mark munched grass. The great Dalrymple lay on his back, his tummy pointing at the sky.

'Sweetie cigarettes?'

'Give it a rest, Derek.' There was a limit to Steve's patience.

'Licorice bootlace?'

'Derek, do shut your mouth – there's a bus comin',' said Tricia.

No doubt about it. They were what Mum and Dad would call 'rough'. They were constantly pushing each other, mauling each other, and telling each other to 'belt up' and 'Stuff it'. Accusations flew – people were 'shamed', 'out of order', 'showed right up'. They kept groaning and pretending they were fed up with each other. Fights broke out: aimless, harmless, pointless fights. Wayne and Mark, for no apparent reason, began to spit chewed grass at each other, then kick each other, then roll over and over, fighting each other.

But Leslie was struck by how much they obviously liked each other. They were friends. They were mates. Wayne and Mark, punching away and laughing. Tricia, shouting at Derek, and laughing at him at the same time. Sharon, spending a great deal of time and effort, trying to upset the Great Dalrymple, by sticking a piece of rye grass up his nose.

If Dad had been there, he would have wanted to organise everyone. 'What's the plan?' That was what Dad always said. 'What's the plan for today?' 'For this afternoon?' 'For next week?'

The Gang didn't have any plans.

As the shadows of the trees lengthened across the playing fields, and the sunlight became more orange than gold, Leslie realized it was getting late.

'Can I have my bicycle?' he said. 'I've got to go now.'

'Give him his bike, Mark,' said Steve. Then, to Leslie, 'Where d'you live, then?'

'143, Parkside Crescent.'

'That's over there, isn't it?' said Steve.

'Yes, you can see the house from here. It's that one, with the red tiles and the white paint.'

'Posh,' said Tricia.

She made it sound like he was 'out of order'.

Chapter 6

143, Parkside Crescent.

He had told them his address.

He had hoped they liked him enough for it to mean something.

He had hoped it meant they would come to his house and invite him out to play.

They didn't.

Perhaps it was all for the best. Again, Mum and Dad were not pleased when he returned late from his meeting with the Gang in the Park.

They tended to blunt the keen feeling of pleasure that he wanted to communicate to them.

'I met these other children...'

'From your school? Now, hurry up and get upstairs. You look very hot and sticky and you need a bath.'

'Not from my school. I don't know where they came from. They were called Steve and Mark...'

'I hope they weren't like those other two.'

'Gary and Lee?' Leslie thought a moment. 'No – nothing like them. And there was Sharon and Tricia . . .'

'While I'm running your bath, you'd better go and get undressed in your room. Hurry up!'

'. . . and the Great Dalrymple . . .'

'Yes, yes. Tell me later. I'm not really listening now.'

'The Great Dalrymple's a skinhead.'

'That doesn't sound very nice.'

'Could I invite them all to a party?'

'What party? You've only just had your birthday. Do hurry up and get in the bath. I can't really hear you in here with the water running.'

It didn't matter. Not a lot. The memory of it all was good enough.

But not for long.

The Gang didn't call for him. Not the next day. And then it was the weekend, and Leslie waited all day long, Saturday, and all day long, Sunday.

Nothing.

It was a relief, almost, to go back to school on Monday. At least there were things to do.

Mrs Hammond had decided that Leslie and Gavin Murchison should do some research into insects. Gavin was a large boy whom Leslie found unbearably dull. The only sign of life in Gavin was his nervousness. He blinked, he twitched, he chewed his nails, he fidgeted. He had no sense of humour and, unfortunately, was terrified of insects. Mrs Hammond knew all this, but she hoped Leslie's intelligence and usual reliability would help Gavin.

She called the two boys up to her desk.

'Your assignment is beetles.'

'Watch they don't crawl in yer earhole, Tubs,' Lee called out, cheerfully, to Gavin.

'Have you learnt those spellings, Lee?'

'Not yet, miss.'

'Better keep quiet, then.' Mrs Hammond looked about her

class as she wrote a note on a piece of paper. It was one of her great skills – to be able to write and keep order at the same time. Leslie watched her, fascinated. It was a skill he greatly admired.

'Take this note to the Library, and ask Mr Emms if you may do your research there. He'll help you find the right books.'

'Miss, do I have to?'

Mrs Hammond smiled at Gavin. She sometimes wondered if Gavin had a looped tape inside his mouth, so that, every time he opened his mouth, out came the words – 'Miss, do I have to?' She had discovered that, year after year, there was always one child in her class that her hands itched to slap. This year that child was Gavin. Her smile, therefore, required considerable effort.

'I think so, Gavin.'

''Ere, Miss?' It was Lee again. 'Didn't Gavin 'ave nits in 'is 'air last term?'

'Get on with your work!'

'I was jus' wond'rin' if that's why you wanted 'im to do insecks. That's all. Jus' wond'rin'.'

Leslie and Gavin went to the Library.

Once he had found the right book, without the help of Mr Emms, Leslie became completely immersed in his work. He liked books. He liked assignments. And he liked insects. While Gavin sat opposite him, nervously turning over the pages of a book about spiders and moaning at each illustration, Leslie read quickly, and made notes about British beetles.

He had no time for Gavin and his hang-ups. He remembered the fuss Gavin had made over 'Charlotte's Web'. Mrs Hammond had read the story to the class, and while he, Leslie, had cried and cried at the description of the death of the spider, Gavin had breathed an audible 'Thank Goodness'.

Still, Gavin's company was at least a relief from loneliness.

For the Gang didn't come that evening. Nor the next. Nor the next. And so it went on until the following weekend came.

* * *

Sunday morning.

'Come on, Leslie,' his dad called. 'We're going to get Nanny.' He sounded a little tired. 'She's going to spend the day with us.'

Nanny lived in an Old People's Home in Lewisham. In a one bedroom flatlet. She said she quite liked it. Most of the time she looked after herself, but there were people about to keep an eye on her. Once a fortnight Dad and Leslie went and fetched her in the car and brought her to Parkside Crescent for the day. Sometimes on a Saturday. Sometimes on a Sunday.

Whichever day it was, they always had a roast dinner and a cooked pudding.

After dinner, while Mum and Dad were busy gardening, Leslie sat on a garden chair next to Nanny.

'Have you got any friends, Nanny?'

'What a funny question, dear.'

'No, it's not. Have you?'

'One or two.'

'Do they call to see you?'

'No.'

'Do you call to see them?'

'No.'

'How do you know they're your friends, then?'

'I see them from time to time. We bump into each other. We have a bit of a chat. I know what to expect from them. I don't like them much, but at least they don't take me by surprise.'

'They sound a bit dull.'

'They're all old, dear. They're hardly likely to do anything exciting. There isn't anything exciting they could do.'

'Nothing?'

'Sometimes they get ill. Or have an accident.'

'That sounds exciting.'

'No, not really. Not like the accidents we used to have in the old days. We had some good old accidents, we did. What was that woman's name? Warrender – Mrs Warrender. She had a grand accident. Cycled into a drinking trough.'

Leslie was intrigued.

'Why?'

'No brakes. And no sense. And you used to get far more food poisoning. Hardly ever get that now.' She sounded disappointed.

'Who do you play with?'

'Play? I don't play. Too old. It's different when you're old.'

'When you were young – did you have friends then?'

'Lots.'

'How many?'

'Lots.'

'What did you do?'

Nanny closed her eyes.

'We used to have lots of arguments.'

'Friends?'

'Course. Lots of rows. We used to make our own fun.'

Here we go again, thought Leslie.

'Where did these friends come from?'

'The street.'

'How did you make these friends?'

'Oh, I can't remember.'

Leslie waited. His Nanny often said that, but she usually could remember. You had go give her time.

'One of my best friends was a girl called Sarah Wycherley. She lived a few doors down on the other side of the street. Number 49. Or was it 59? 57?'

There were some things Leslie knew Nanny wouldn't remember. He had to interrupt her.

'Tell me about how you made friends with her.'

'Who, dear?'

'This girl. Sarah.'

'The milkcart used to stop outside our house, and in those days, you took a jug out for your milk and the milkman ladled it from a big churn.'

Leslie listened very patiently to an account of old London life that he had heard several times before.

Nanny beamed at him. 'Can you imagine that, eh?'

'Yes,' said Leslie, a little impatiently. 'Yes, I can. We did an assignment at school on street traders.'

'The things they teach nowadays,' said Nanny. She made it sound as if the school had trodden on her toes. Well, she wasn't going to sit back and let them take over her store of golden memories.

'We didn't 'ave bottles. No, what d'you call them? – cartons. No cartons, neither. Little milkcart and the milkman pushing it. I suppose your school told you the cart was pulled by a horse.'

'No,' said Leslie. 'Pushcart – like you said.'

Nanny's mouth began to twitch.

'It weren't pasteurised. The milk. Not pasteurised. There was a little signboard on the side of the cart. "Fresh milk – warm from the cow". I give your great granma a scare. Pretended the milk was so warm, it burnt me mouth.' Nanny laughed.

'Go on about friends.' The afternoon was passing, but Nanny would not be hurried.

'There was another sign – front of the cart. "E. I. Williamson, Springfield Farm Dairy. Absolutely Pure Milk From Our Cows". And, on the back of the cart – "Alderney Cows Kept For Infants And Invalids". Lies. All of it. We all knew Ernie Williamson. Only farm he'd ever been to was Chalk Farm Railway Depot. And that was what was in his milk: chalk, flour, water, powder – Ernie put everything in his milk.' There was a light of challenge in Nanny's eyes. Let them put that in their fancy school assignments!

She settled back in her chair.

'Well, go on!' said Leslie.

'What, dear?'

'About Sarah!'

Nanny's mouth sagged open.

Leslie read this as a sign that she needed prompting.

'Sarah Wycherley. You were telling me how you made friends with her.'

Nanny closed her mouth and nodded.

'That's right. Well, now, everyday Sarah used to take her jug and wait at the milkcart at the same time that I took our jug. So, after a few days I decided it was only right and proper and manners to say something to her.'

'What did you say?'

'I think I said: "You look as though you've not washed your face this week."'

Leslie frowned. It didn't sound like a promising beginning to a friendship.

He discussed this later with Lennie and Luke Skywalker.

'Would you want to be friends with someone who said that to you?'

Luke was slowly climbing over a cabbage leaf. Lennie was giving his teeth an airing.

'Mind you,' went on Leslie, 'she did say it takes time. Her and this girl. It was days and days before they said anything nice to each other. But then, they had plenty of time. They saw each other every day.'

He thought a moment.

'It's no good saying I see people at school every day.'

It wasn't obvious that either Lennie or Luke was about to say that.

'Don't have time to make friends there. Mrs Hammond keeps us too busy. And they're all friends before I ever got there. They made friends when they were First Years.'

He fitted a full water bottle against the netting side of Lennie's hutch.

He thought of the Gang.

'I just wish they'd come.'

Chapter 7

The Gang didn't come, but Lee and Gary did. There was something about Leslie that fascinated and attracted them. He was smart, got all his work right, knew about all sorts of things. But that wasn't it.

It was his innocence. As far as they could see, Leslie never did anything wrong. Never got into trouble. Never got told off. Could anyone be that good? They had decided to put him to the test.

They called early one Saturday morning. Very early.

There was a loud knocking on the door.

Leslie put on his towelling bathrobe and rushed downstairs. He hoped it was the postman with a parcel.

He opened the door.

Lee and Gary were poised at the gate, ready for flight. They had feared Leslie's Mum or Dad might answer.

'What's the matter?'

'Get your clothes on, Leslie, and get down the Park as quick as you can. By the swings. Quick as you can!'

'All right, Leslie?'

'An' you better be there!' Lee added a late threat, and then he and Gary raced away down the Crescent.

A threat – yes. But an invitation too. Leslie knew he'd regret it afterwards if he didn't go.
So he went.
He dressed quickly in his bedroom, went downstairs, and opened the front door.
He called upstairs.
'Mum! Dad! All right if I go in the Park before breakfast?'
He counted to three – as fast as he could – and rushed out slamming the door behind him.
That was all right. He had *asked* them, hadn't he? And the door slamming must have woken them up. So, if there was any argument afterwards, he could claim that he thought they knew he was out.
It wouldn't do any good, any of it, but it was 'a leg to stand on'. Dad was always going on about Leslie not having 'a leg to stand on' in these arguments.

Leslie ran along the Crescent and then down Parkside Road. He entered the Park from the Downham end, the gate nearest to the children's playground.
Gary and Lee were where they had said they would be, by the swings, and with them was another, bigger boy.
They beckoned to Leslie.
As he approached, Leslie saw that the older boy looked more like a 'youth'. He was taller than Gary or Lee. Thinner. His features were harsher, his nose bonier, his eyes narrower, his mouth grimmer. His lips were pressed so tightly together there scarcely seemed room to insert the cigarette he was smoking. His curly hair was coiled tight, and had the wiry look of metal rings. And he wore dark glasses.
Leslie felt sorry for him. Perhaps he had hay fever. Leslie's Mum sometimes wore dark glasses when she had hay fever and the pollen count was high.
But there was something harsh, cutting, scary about him.

'Me brother Craig,' said Lee, making the introductions. 'I've told 'im who you are.'

'Hi Leslie,' murmured Craig. 'You cool?'

'No thanks. I've got my pyjamas on under my sweater.' Well, thought Leslie, appearances can be deceptive. Here was Craig looking all tough, and he was actually worried whether Leslie was warm enough.

Craig's lip curled as he squeezed the cigarette back into his mouth. He turned to Lee.

'Some kind of joker, is he?'

'No, Craig, no. 'E's smart, Leslie. Aintcha smart!'

'All right, Leslie?' Gary put on his goofy smile.

'Only this has gotta be water-tight. No chances. No slip-ups.' Craig looked about him. The Park was empty. 'Right, then, 'ere's the scenario.'

At his feet was a sack. Craig picked it up.

Scenario, thought Leslie. Funny name for a sack.

From the sack Craig took out a large bundle of newspapers. He divided them into three piles.

'Now get this. These go out at retail, right? No back-of-the-lorry discount for the punters on these. Otherwise every dimmo about will know they're hot. It's up to you to find the right location. I'm right out of it. Your split's fifty per cent gross and we meet back 'ere, 'alf ten. Got it?'

Lee and Gary nodded.

Leslie hadn't the faintest idea what Craig was talking about. Retail? Cool? Hot? Back-of-the-lorry? Gross? What did it all mean? What did *any* of it mean? But he was too nervous and too shy to ask. It seemed best to nod like the others and pretend to know. A bit like doing PE.

Craig hunched his silver bomber jacket round his shoulders and began to slope off.

'Don't you want your scenario?' Leslie called, waving the sack.

Lee snatched it from him.

'I'm 'avin' that,' he said. 'OK, Leslie. No time to waste. That lot's yours an' you gotta get it sold quick.'

So that was it.

Like a newspaper round, only you had to go out and find the customers. Leslie glanced at the top of the papers. Yes, they were today's papers. That was easy, then. Just find the right place to sell them.

It was even more like a newspaper round than he imagined, for Craig had stolen the papers from a delivery boy only an hour earlier. Leslie, however, was not to know this.

'Get goin', Leslie. See you half ten.'

Gary and Lee were off.

The bundle was heavy. Leslie staggered over the bridge, across the Park, and out of the gates nearest his house.

No point in taking the papers home. He couldn't sell them all there.

At the very back of his mind Leslie had a suspicion that there was something dishonest in what he was doing, but he chose to ignore the very-back-of-his-mind.

Papers.

Where would be a good place to sell papers?

The railway station. People were always reading papers on the train! That would be just the place.

Leslie balanced his bundle on his shoulder, crossed the main road that ran past the Park, and staggered down the alleyway to Beckenham Hill Station.

There was a large car parking area outside the station, and there Leslie set up, ready for business.

His methodical mind set to work.

He undid the string round his bundle and sorted the papers into different piles, Mail, Mirror, Sun, Telegraph, Express. There were only a couple of copies of the Times and the Guardian, and these he put together.

He could not help noticing that all the papers had numbers and letters pencilled on the top right hand corners of the front pages.

    23 PC   14 Hed. Rd.
    76 PC   32 Hed. Rd.

```
 83 PC      39 Hed. Rd.
143 PC     159 Oakl.
```

The very-back-of-his-mind took a step forward. Leslie began to worry, and to hope he would be able to get rid of the papers quickly.

He waited.

No one came into the station approach.

It was Saturday. There were no commuters. There were very few trains. The service on Saturday was limited to one train every half hour. He had just missed one. It was too early for shoppers who might want to go northbound to Peckham Rye, or southbound to Bromley South.

A few birds sang.

On the main road cars passed – and the occasional motor-bike.

From the flats in Dunfield Road came the noise of a jubilant stereo music centre.

A light breeze arose, fluttering the pages of the newspapers. Leslie looked around for weights to secure them. Under some spindly elder bushes growing in an untended corner was a heap of broken bricks.

He placed a piece of broken brick on each pile of papers. Then he thought it would look neater if he placed bits of brick at each corner of each pile.

There were lots of bits of brick.

And still, no one came.

Perhaps he could find enough bits of brick to write the names of the papers on their respective piles.

'The Sun' was easy enough. So was 'The Star'. 'The Express' took a lot more bricks, and by the time he got to 'Daily Mail', he had lost interest.

He had no idea what the time was, but he reckoned it must be near half past ten. There would probably be a clock in the station lobby. Leslie went in to check.

Eight fifteen!

Hours to go.

This was very boring.

Where else did people buy papers?

Of course, at paper shops!

There was one in Downham, the other side of the Park. By the traffic lights. The one that Lee and Gary were banned from.

He kicked the bricks back under the elder bushes and gathered up his newspapers. The top copies were now a little grubby, but he hoped he could fold them a special way so that people wouldn't notice. He tied the string on the bundle.

He went back up the alleyway, over the main road, and back into the Park. There was no sign of Gary, Lee or Craig, but there were a few grown-ups, exercising their dogs.

It was a long walk, right through to the Downham side, along Old Bromley Road, across the lights at Downham Way, and past the shops to the newsagents.

What a terrible fuss!

How was he to know the papers were stolen! How was he to know the delivery boy they were stolen from worked for that newsagent!

His confession had been immediate and complete. He told the newsagent all about Gary, Lee and Craig – omitting only their names. He told him about the arrangement to meet in the Park at half past ten. The newsagent believed in swift justice and not involving the police. He informed Leslie he would accompany him home, tell Leslie's parents all about it, and would then lie in wait, in the Park, to catch the other three boys. The newsagent was particularly interested in Craig.

Leslie's Mum and Dad were shocked, horrified, upset, hurt, indignant, embarrassed – almost everything Leslie didn't want them to be. They said they would deal with him later, and the newsagent dragged a tearful Leslie into the Park.

'You wait by those swings, and when your mates come – don't you dare say a thing about me. I'm hiding here.' The newsagent crouched under the playground slide.

A quarter of an hour later, Gary entered the Park. He still had most of his bundle of newspapers. He saw Leslie and hurried over.

'All right, Leslie?' The goofy smile. The usual greeting.

'Yes,' said Leslie. But his voice sounded stiff and thick. It was fortunate that Gary was too dim to notice that something was very wrong.

Two minutes dragged by – Lee came into the Park. He had sold all his papers. He waved to Gary and Leslie.

'Done all right,' he called. As he ran up there could hear lots of small change clinking in his bulging pockets.

''Ere,' said Lee, surprised and impressed, 'you got rid of yours an' all, Leslie. Smart. Craig'll be pleased.'

On the stroke of half past ten, Craig made his entrance. He had already given this moment some thought, and wanted it to be dramatic. He was now on a bicycle – a machine with large wheels, no mudguards, a small frame, and vast cow-horn handlebars. He was still smoking. He rode up – no hands on the handlebars.

If he had not had his dark glasses on, he might have seen the newsagent stir under the slide. A slight attack of cramp.

He might also have seen Leslie's parents, unable to keep away, approaching in the distance.

'Pay-off time,' said Craig. 'You done good, boys. Real good. I'll maybe use you again.'

'All right, Craig?' said Gary.

'Give us the tosh, and I'll give you your cut.'

That was the moment when the newsagent sprang and Leslie's parents hurried over the bridge.

The newsagent missed Craig, but grabbed hold of Gary's sweater. He swung round and grabbed Lee's arm with his other hand. Leslie stood, unable to move, rooted to the spot.

But Craig was off. The cigarette fell from his mouth, the dark glasses fell off his nose, and he very nearly fell off his bicycle. Wobble, wobble, wobble, but somehow he managed to stay on, and, faster than Leslie would have thought possible, Craig sped away.

His entry had been dramatic, his exit was more so. He just

missed a Jack Russell terrier, so closely that its owner aimed a blow at Craig with the dog's lead; swerved past a woman pushing a pram; went right through the paddling pool; scraped along the side of the refreshment kiosk; bumped over the grass, and disappeared in the direction of Downham.

Gary and Lee struggled in the newsagent's grip, but neither effectively nor hopefully.

'Turn your pockets out,' he ordered.

The coins fell on the grass at their feet.

'You! Count it.'

While Mum and Dad watched from a little way off, Leslie arranged the money in stacks – ten ps, five ps, two ps. Like they did the play money in the Infants. But this was real money and real life and real trouble.

'Twelve pounds forty eight pence,' he said.

'Didn't we do well?' said Gary.

'That the lot?' The newsagent shook Gary and Lee, as though expecting stray coins to drop from their clothes.

Nothing.

'Right. Whose idea?'

Leslie shook his head.

'Not mine,' said Gary.

'Not mine,' said Lee.

'Who was that on the bike?'

Silence.

More shaking.

'Who was that on the bike?'

'Never seen 'im before. You let me go. I'll get my Dad up 'ere.' Lee was recovering his nerve.

The newsagent shook, shouted and threatened. Leslie wanted to tell him who Craig was, but daren't.

Gradually the newsagent became calmer. He had recovered half his newspapers and the money for the other half. He had frightened the culprits, including the ringleader, and he might as well call it a day. There was work to be done. These papers should be delivered as soon as possible. It was time he returned to his shop.

'Right,' growled the newsagent, 'if ever I see any of you lads again, there'll be trouble. I mean that. And, if anyone so much as looks at my delivery boys or girls, I'll find him and I'll give him a good hiding. It's only since I've got the papers back and the money that I don't give you a good hiding now. So clear off!'

As Lee and Gary hastened away, all dignity gone, Gary picked something up from the grass.

'Your brother left his sunglasses,' he said to Lee.

'Shut up, dimmo!'

'Right. You can tell your brother I'll be round to see him,' said the newsagent.

Gary and Lee left the Park. Leslie stood where he was.

The newsagent looked at him, and then across at his mum and dad.

'You can go,' he said, more gently. 'Your mum and dad will have more to say to you.'

That was undoubtedly true.

'I've got what I wanted, and those two have got what they deserved.' The newsagent picked up his money and papers.

Leslie wanted to be helpful.

'If I find the scenario, I'll bring it round to the shop.'

The newsagent frowned and gazed at Leslie's back as he walked away.

'Loony kids,' he muttered.

Mum and Dad did indeed have more to say. Hours and hours of it. All that Saturday. Morning, lunchtime, afternoon. And Nanny was dragged into it, and the more they nagged, the more upset and angry Leslie became.

It was all a mistake.

All right, all right – yes, they had told him not to have anything to do with Lee and Gary – thirty six times, they'd told him that.

Sarcastic? No, he wasn't being sarcastic. He was simply pointing out how many times they'd told him not to have anything to do with . . .

Yes, yes, yes, he *did* know it was wrong. But he hadn't known that at first.

Oh yes, he had told them he was going out to the Park before breakfast!

No, of course he wouldn't ever do anything like this again.

What did they mean 'possessed him'? Nothing 'possessed him'. It was this youth and the scenario and re-telling and front-of-lorries and outlets per centre. No – it didn't much make sense to him, either.

No, he didn't want to go to prison – though perhaps he'd get a bit of peace and quiet there, and people wouldn't go on at him so much.

No, he wasn't trying to be funny.

Yes, he *was* sorry.

He was. Very sorry. Mum would be all right, eventually. But he expected Dad to go on all weekend. Dad got into such a state.

When he went to bed that evening, Leslie was still feeling guilty and miserable. He heard Mum and Dad talking downstairs. Usually he liked people to talk about him. He had overheard many complimentary remarks in the past. Tonight he guessed what they were saying would be less pleasant. They might even be planning to send him away. Those schools where bad children went. Boarding schools! Or they might have him 'done away with' in a Children's Home.

The thought was unbearable, but he had to know what they were saying. He slipped from his bed, and tip-toed to the top of the stairs. He came down the stairs backwards – he had learnt by experiment that you could be far quieter coming downstairs backwards than forwards. Halfway down he stopped and listened. He could hear quite clearly what Mum and Dad were saying.

'He doesn't seem to know what he's doing half the time.' That was Dad.

'He's all right. And I'm sure this morning must have been a dreadful fright for him.'

'For him! What about us? I only hope the neighbours don't get to hear about it.' Dad was worked up. Leslie heard the noise of a bottle being opened and drink poured into a glass.

'Didn't you ever do anything wrong when you were a child?' said Mum.

'Of course I did. But we're talking about stolen goods here. Stolen goods! And the explanation he offered! Incredible! All that talk about "scenarios" and "centres". Could *you* understand it? And then, a few weeks back, there was that talk about eating bicycles! and chemists. I'm not saying he's mad, but, well, maybe we should get someone to have a look at him.'

It was Leslie's turn to be baffled.

'The one I'd like to get hold of,' said Mum, 'is the youth. He's the one who pinched the papers from the delivery boy in the first place. He's the one who started the whole thing.'

'Monstrous,' said Dad. 'I don't know what we're coming to. No thought for people. We're producing a generation of young thugs who couldn't care less.'

Leslie hadn't realised how tired he was, how big a strain the day had been. He yawned – a long, big yawn. A noisy yawn.

Mum came out of the living room.

'You're supposed to be in bed,' she said. 'Come on, up you go.' And she helped him upstairs and tucked him into his bed.

She sat on the bed, beside him, and stroked his hair. Her hand was soft, gentle, very reassuring.

'No more silliness,' she said. 'No more adventures with Gary and Lee. They're not your sort.'

Leslie's eyes began to close.

'And keep well away from the Craigs of this world. They're bad through and through.'

A last spark of consciousness flickered in Leslie's mind.

'Craig can't be absolutely bad,' he murmured. 'He did want to know if I was cold.'

Chapter 8

Leslie was in his bedroom, sulking.

To start with, it was Wednesday, the day his class was *supposed* to go swimming. And they hadn't. Mrs Hammond said it was because the Swimming Instructress at the Baths was ill. Typical!

He stared out of his bedroom window, beyond the garden, over to the Park.

It was late July, the last week of term. A damp, overcast, hazy, muggy day. Tempers had been short at school, and, although the affair of Craig and the newspapers had blown over, short at home. The trees along the river and in the far woods were dark green, but with a dusting of blue and grey powder. The grass was yellowing with the passing summer, the earth darkened by recent rain.

It all looked very still.

Leslie noticed some figures moving across the humpback bridge.

One, two, three, four, five . . .

Was it the Gang?

'. . . six, seven, eight.'

The figures stopped.

Must be. Must be! That was Tilt, leaning slightly to one side. And the fat one – the Great Dalrymple.

What were they doing?

He wanted to go and see.

He raced downstairs.

'Mum, Mum!' Why didn't she answer at once?

'Mum!'

'*What?*'

'Can I go and play in the Park?'

'I thought you were sulking?'

'Thanks, Mum.'

Leslie slammed the front door shut. He ran along the lane that led to the garages behind the houses, wriggled through a gap in the fence and was in the Park.

It was the Gang.

They were standing in a circle.

He heard the Great Dalrymple say: 'Now,' and then they all fell down.

He heard them laugh.

As he got nearer he heard Mark say: 'Here comes Les.'

Tricia said: 'Good. He can help. The more the merrier.'

The Great Dalrymple was organising them. 'Get up. Come on, Derek. Get up.'

'It's my leg,' said Derek. 'I think it's broken. Ten minutes to go in the final of the World Cup and England's striker's down with a broken leg, scores are 2-all. Will he be able to complete his hat-trick with a broken leg?'

''Ere, Derek, if I give you 5p will you go away?' It was Tricia.

The Great Dalrymple was getting cross and sweaty. 'Derek, shut up a moment and stand *there*. Wayne, you – here. Tilt – over here.'

Eventually he had them all in a circle, almost touching.

'Now it *ought* to work.'

'The Great Dalrymple has spoken,' said Mark.

Leslie still didn't know what was happening.

Sharon was in front of Leslie and Wayne was behind him.

'Now,' said the Great Dalrymple.

Sharon bent her legs and leaned backwards as though trying to sit on Leslie. Because he wasn't prepared for this, he hadn't bent *his* legs to make a lap for her to sit on.

Sharon fell over.

So did Tilt, who was in front of her, and Steve, who was in front of Tilt, and so on, round the circle, until only Leslie was left standing.

The others sat on the grass and looked at him.

'Why did you do that?' said Mark.

''S like Ring-a-Ring-a-Roses, innit?' said Tricia.

'Could 'ave killed us all,' muttered Derek.

The Great Dalrymple fumed.

'It works if *everybody* joins in. But *one*,' his eyes were on Leslie, '*one* can wreck it.'

The guinea pig feeling rose up in Leslie.

'Hang about,' Steve interrupted. 'Did anyone tell you what we're trying to do?'

'No,' said Leslie.

'So tell him,' Steve said to the Great Dalrymple.

'It's a Sitting Circle. Each person sits on the lap of the person behind, and you form a great big circle with everyone sitting down.'

'We ain't got enough people,' said Sharon.

''E can't manage what we 'ave got,' said Tricia.

'Would anybody else like Fatty to sit on them,' said Derek, ''e's like a bloomin' 'ippo.'

The Great Dalrymple ignored this rudeness. 'We shall try once more,' he said.

They tried once more.

It worked.

They sat there, each one on the lap of the person behind. In a circle. There were a few moans and groans, particularly from Derek, but after about ten seconds, they each realized how silly they looked.

They started laughing.

Then they realized how difficult it was to laugh and keep the Sitting Circle going.

They wobbled and giggled and giggled and wobbled.

'Keep STILL!' shouted the Great Dalrymple, though he was laughing and shaking more than anyone else.

'The Earth,' gasped Derek, 'it's opening up beneath me . . . I can't . . . aaargh!!'

He collapsed, and, like a circle of dominoes falling one on another, one by one they all tumbled.

They lay on the ground, laughing.

After a while Mark said: 'The ground's wet. I'm getting up.'

'Just as well,' said Tricia, ''cos there's a beetle crawlin' up your leg.'

Mark leapt up, shaking his legs. He stopped, and carefully searched the ground around him. 'You havin' me on?'

'No,' said Tricia. 'Though I like the dance you done – any chance of an encore?'

For a while Leslie and the Gang continued to lie on the grass, gazing at the sky, talking aimlessly, watching visitors to the Park stroll by – the 'doggers' and the 'joggers', the 'talkers' and the 'walkers'. Then, for some, boredom set in.

The atmosphere was getting heavier, the clouds thicker. Thunder was in the air.

'We've played Philip's silly game,' said Tilt. 'We gonna 'ang about all day?'

The Great Dalrymple stuck his tongue out at her.

'Charmin'! I'm fed up. I'm goin'. You comin', Tricia?' Tilt moved away towards the humpback bridge over the river.

'Let's go and fish.' It was one of Steve's less inspiring suggestions.

'We're always doing that,' said Mark. 'I'm going up the shops.'

'Where?'

'Bolter's.'

That was the newsagent. *The* newsagent. Not enough time

had passed yet for Leslie to have recovered from that Saturday escapade. He couldn't help remembering it, and, each time, he felt bad.

'Who's comin' up Bolters? Steve? Sharon? Les?'

'I can't,' said Leslie. 'Not allowed.'

'Your mum and dad won't mind.'

'Not Mum and Dad. I've been banned from Bolters.'

The Gang didn't believe him.

'Banned? You banned from Bolters? Whatever you done, Les?'

'You wasn't behind the great Mars Bar Heist, was you?' Derek was particularly excited.

Les explained. And as he explained he realized there were some funny sides to the story. He began to present the story as a bit of a laugh. He exaggerated Gary's goofiness, the wild manner of Craig's departure from the Park, Lee's struggles in the grip of the newsagent.

Steve and Sharon laughed a lot. Derek's mouth sagged open.

'Les – how could you? How *could* you?'

'You sound like my Dad,' said Leslie, smiling broadly.

'But it was me!' went on Derek. 'It was me they robbed. It was my paper round. My papers they took. Four of them. Masked. The leader had a sawn off shot gun.'

'Sawn off catapult, more like,' said Sharon.

'I put up a fantastic struggle, knocked four of 'em out, but the leader conked me with 'is gun on the side of the 'ead, and I blacked out.'

Leslie was appalled.

Sharon took on what was normally Tilt's role. 'It's all lies,' she said. ''E left his sack of papers outside the Gents in the Woodland Walk, and when 'e come out, they was gone.'

'There was *one*. And 'e 'adn't gone. Kicked me on the shin so 'ard, I couldn't run after 'im. Still got the bruise.' Derek rolled up his trouser leg.

'Oooo,' said Sharon. 'Lovely bit of leg, Derek. Lovely! Does Tilt know 'ow 'andsome you are?'

'I'm ever so sorry,' said Leslie.

'Why? You didn't kick him,' said Steve. 'Anyway, kicking's good for the circulation.'

'Not newspaper circulation, it ain't,' said Derek.

'I'm not 'angin' about admirin' Derek's legs,' said Mark. 'I'm goin' up the shops. See you.'

He moved away, in the direction taken by Tilt and Tricia.

There was a flash of lightning.

'Thunder Gods angry. Make sky split in two. Bits of it probably fall on heads of wrongdoers.' It was Derek. He looked at Leslie. 'That's you, Les. Gettin' involved with gangs of vicious thugs. Tryin' to kill innocent newspaper boys.'

'Loony,' said Sharon. 'An' I'm not stayin' 'ere with a crowd of loonies, waitin' to get rained on.'

The crack of thunder snapped through the Park.

Wayne shivered. 'See you,' he said and ran after Sharon.

There was another lightning flash, and a much shorter pause before the thunder.

'The storm's getting nearer,' said Leslie.

'How do you make that out?'

So even Steve didn't know everything.

'The flash of lightning travels faster than the noise of thunder. So, although they happen at the same time, the further they have to travel to reach you, the longer the gap between them. It's like when Derek was riding my bicycle the other day. He said he was going faster than the speed of sound . . .'

'And then faster than the speed of light,' the Great Dalrymple interrupted. 'Yeah, I see.'

The first few big drops of rain began to fall. The sky was very dark.

'There's goin' to be a flood,' said Derek. 'The river will overflow. The whole park will be under what-d'you-call-it, fathoms, fathoms of surging rain. Houses will be washed away. We shall have to swim to the Post Office Tower.'

Steve, Leslie and the Great Dalrymple took no notice. Derek felt very disappointed.

'Isn't anybody goin' to tell me to shut up?'

There was more lightning and thunder. The rain spattered across the grass, staining the ground.

'I'd better go home,' said Leslie.

'Let's run,' said Steve.

They ran.

Leslie found it hard to keep up with them. He had things on his mind. Perhaps the Gang wouldn't want to have anything more to do with him now they knew of his part in the newspaper business?

Then he recalled what Nanny had said about the girl with the milkcart. Sarah. Nanny had said it was days and days before she said anything pleasant to Sarah. And yet, Sarah had ended up Nanny's friend.

Perhaps it was all right. Perhaps you could have rows.

It was raining heavily now.

'I'm going home,' said Steve. 'See you, Les.'

Steve, Derek and the Great Dalrymple hurried away.

For a moment Leslie watched them go. His clothes were already wet. It was getting gloomier and colder. He felt low in spirits, and yet sort of angry.

There'd be a row when he got home.

Chapter 9

He was right. There was a row.

He was told, sharply, to go upstairs and change.

He went upstairs and stood, in his dripping clothes, gazing out of his bedroom window at the Park.

The storm was even nearer now. Lightning and thunder sparkled and crackled almost simultaneously. Everything looked dark and thick, like a great blanket flung over the Park, hot, sticky and suffocating.

But the storm seemed determined to tear the blanket to shreds, to rip it, to rend it, to stab through it.

It was exhilirating.

The rain was pouring down, bouncing off the roof of the garden shed, bouncing off the garages, beating down the flowers and the grass, crushing the tall weeds that grew along the edge of the park – cow parsley and rose bay willow herb.

'Blimey,' said Leslie, to himself, but out loud.

He felt cheered by the storm. It was good, it was powerful, it was exciting.

More lightning, more thunder. More rain.

* * *

More shouting from downstairs.

'Have you got your wet clothes off yet?'

Leslie gave himself just enough time to whip off two wet socks (clothes) before he answered, in a slightly testy voice:

'Yes!'

'Then hurry up and come down for your tea.'

'Up' and 'down'.

Huh!

He wasn't going to sulk any more. He was going to rebel. To be tough. They weren't going to boss him about. No way. He'd *change*. If a caterpillar could become a butterfly, he didn't see why a guinea pig shouldn't become a lion.

He looked at himself in the mirror and snarled.

His mother called up. 'There, see, now you've caught a cold.'

'I haven't.'

'I heard you sneeze.'

'That wasn't a sneeze, it was a . . .'

It didn't seem right, somehow, that the King of the Beasts should have to explain what he was doing.

He'd show them.

He'd . . .

What would he do?

Build a helicopter?

He couldn't.

Do a hundred metre Wheelie?

Huh, he couldn't.

He remembered a trip to the Zoo with his class in the Infants. Other children had gone on and on about the chimpanzees and the bear cubs and the Reptile House. But not him. He had watched the lions.

That look of superiority in their eyes. They looked as if they owned the Zoo, not as if they were captives. The bulging, rippling muscles. The great soft feet, about as soft really as a boxing glove with a hammer punch inside it. The 'licensed-to-kill' teeth. Above all, the haughty patience: waiting, waiting, as though some day they reckoned they were bound to escape. And then? Then the world would have to look out.

'Your tea's getting cold, and I'm getting fed up waiting.'

What a way to talk to the King of the Beasts! His Mum and Dad had better watch out! Let them come to the waterhole tonight to brush their teeth! He'd leap on their backs and sink his claws into the backs of their necks.

Leaping. He wasn't too sure how good he was at that. It was Sports Day tomorrow. He'd have a go at leaping in the Long Jump and see how he got on. Best to find out before he went for the kill. I mean, it would be awful to lie on a branch in a tree, in the park, by the river, waiting for some show-off cyclist to come down to drink, and then leap out, miss, and fall into the river. Like he'd done on his bicycle.

That still hurt.

The memory of that awful flop into the river. Dropping like a fat stone! Good job no one saw.

In his imagination, standing by the window, gazing at the rain drenched park, he had this picture of Leslie the Lion, on his bicycle, leaping over the river.

Now that *would* show them.

He liked that idea.

Leslie's Leap.

He thought about it at the tea table. Sailing over the river, over the nettles and the thistles on the other bank, and landing triumphantly on the grass on the other side. Riding a little way, while the cheers rang out, and then slewing the bicycle round, coming to rest, and getting off while they patted his back.

'Do look where your food's going,' said Dad, in the tone of voice which shouldn't be used to a hero and daredevil. 'It's supposed to go in your mouth, not down your trousers.'

Daredevil. Devil! That was the word.

Like Evil Knievel. Daring – and more than a bit flash.

No more the guinea pig!

A daredevil.

A superman.

The King of the Beasts.

Tea was over.

'You haven't given your guinea pig any food today,' said Mum. 'And it needs fresh water.'

The King of the Beasts mooched sulkily down the garden to water his guinea pig.

Huh!

Chapter 10

Yes, but how?

That was the point.

How?

He wasn't sure how wide the stream was. And he had no idea how far you could leap on a bicycle.

He had tried to bring the subject up, casually, at school.

'Evil Knievel wouldn't be able to jump over many barrels on a Chopper, would he?'

Derision!

They made fun of him!

'Evil Knievel don't *jump* over anything!'

'He leaps!'

'An' 'e don't leap over barrels, mate. It's *buses*!'

'Like to see 'im leap a bus on a Chopper!'

Much laughter.

Leslie, feeling dreadful, persisted.

'But, if he did . . .'

'More likely Evil Knievel could leap a bus over a Chopper.'

'But if he was riding a Chopper . . .' He was near to tears. It seemed they were all dancing around him, making fun of him, mobbing him. All a blur. Their voices came from every angle. He couldn't keep up with it.

He ran from them.

All right, then. He'd go to Miss Hammond. She was supposed to know so much. All that research.

He found her in his classroom. She was talking to Miss Tilley, the part-time Music teacher.

He waited by Mrs Hammond's table.

The conversation between the two teachers died suddenly.

Miss Hammond smiled at Leslie. Miss Tilley's face gave what was meant to be a friendly sort of twitch.

'Yes, Leslie?'

'Miss, about Evil Knievel.'

Mrs Hammond was a good teacher. She worked hard to keep abreast of junior culture. She had been well informed about Evil Knievel in the days when he had a lot of publicity, and she could recall enough about him.

'What about Evil Knievel?'

'Miss, he had a motorbike, but could he have done as well with a pedal cycle? Like mine?'

'I don't think so.' Mrs Hammond looked straight at him. 'It's a question of speed, you see. The faster you go, the further you can leap. You watch them at the Long Jump this afternoon. Good long jumpers have to be good sprinters. And no pedal bike can go as fast as a motorbike.'

Every sentence of Mrs Hammond's produced a beam and a nod from Miss Tilley. She, too, was looking straight at Leslie, and fidgeting slightly on her feet, like a bird moving along a perch.

Leslie didn't like Miss Tilley. He ignored her beams and nods and kept his attention rigidly on Mrs Hammond.

'So, Miss, how far can an ordinary bicycle leap?'

'I've really no idea – only a very short distance. Perhaps a metre.'

A metre?

That was no good.

His face must have showed disappointment.

'How far did you want to jump?'

'Oh, it's not me, Miss. It's . . . it's a friend. My friend, er, Luke – (emphatically) You don't know him. He wants to leap on a bicycle.'

'And ride off into the sunset?' said Mrs Hammond, smiling gently.

Leslie was already too confused to take any notice. Even while battling with embarrassment and not very effective deceit he had this mental picture of Luke, his tortoise, trying to ride a bicycle.

'So, er, I just wondered.'

There was a pause.

Mrs Hammond was still smiling.

Miss Tilley was still hopping up and down her perch, hoping someone would chuck her a couple of sunflower seeds.

'Thanks, Miss. I'll go now.'

'Leslie!'

It was old Tilley, calling him back.

'Yes, Miss?'

'Wouldn't you like to join my little group of Multi-Ethnic Songsters this term?'

'No, I wouldn't.'

'Leslie!'

He hadn't meant to sound that rude – it was his disappointment at being told all he could hope for was a leap of one puny metre.

But it was Mrs Hammond who had noticed his rudeness. Miss Tilley continued, unaware.

She had two vacancies in her song group – places until recently filled by Lee and Gary.

Gary and Lee had joined the Songsters because 'old Tilley's classes were always good for a laugh'. They had managed to turn her attempts to rehearse an Indian Rice Planting Song into a frenzied re-enactment of Custer's Last Stand. For 'Indians' meant only one thing to Gary and Lee. Miss Tilley had given up the Rice Planting Song. She hadn't really minded. All the children had found it very hard to sing bent over double, miming the planting of rice. But she had decided to do without Gary and Lee.

Leslie, on the other hand, was a different sort of boy. Trustworthy. Reliable. Quiet. A touch 'dolce'. A touch 'pianissimo'. There was something unavoidably 'forte' about everything Lee did.

'We shall be singing such a lovely collection of songs. Some West Indian calypsos, and a Christmas Carol from Finland, and a Maori canoe-ing song . . .'

Miss Tilley hadn't expected to hold Leslie's attention for long – she never did with children – and she was now directing her remarks at Mrs Hammond.

'. . . and a clapping song from Ruanda-Urundi, or is it called something else now? I can't keep up. All these coups and independencies. I really do wish some of these African countries would stabilise. They make it very difficult for those of us of a Multi-Ethnic persuasion. Anyway, there's a herdsman's song from Mongolia . . .'

Leslie nipped smartly out of the classroom.

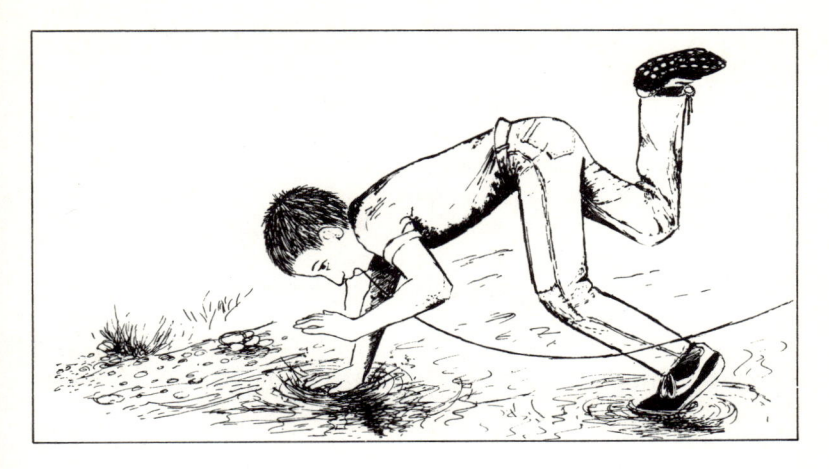

Chapter 11

It was the last week of July, and the first week of the summer holidays.

It was hot.

It had been sunny for several days, and there had been no recent rain.

The river was short of water.

It was shallower than usual – and, in many places, much narrower than usual.

About the best time, Leslie reckoned, for leaping.

He had tried to get a conversation going with Nanny, after Sunday lunch, the day before.

'Nanny, I'm going to be famous.'

'Of course, dear,' said Nanny, without taking her eyes from an old Bing Crosby film on television. She was feeling very content. Leslie's mum and dad were in the garden and not pestering her. She was full of roast chicken and apple pie. And she'd always liked Bing Crosby films.

'I'm going to do something that will surprise everyone.'

'Mm.'

'It's very, very exciting. I don't want you to tell Mum and Dad. Not yet.'

Even a lion, presumably, had trouble with its parents. Gets lugged around in their mouths, and bashed about a lot.

So this would be better as a secret between him and Nanny. Nanny wasn't very interested.

'I shall be risking life and limb,' said Leslie.

Nanny never took her eyes from the television.

'This bit is where the horse dies at the end of the race. Makes you cry,' said Nanny, happily.

'I may well be crippled, should I fall.' She still wasn't listening. Sucking strong peppermints and gazing at that rubbishy old film.

'Nanny!'

'More like a friend than a horse.'

That had been yesterday. Now, Monday morning, Leslie was by himself, on the river bank.

He was by himself because he didn't have any friends, and he was on the river bank because he was trying to measure how wide the river was.

He had tied one end of a piece of string to a stick, and shoved the stick into the river bank. The other end of the piece of string was weighted with a stone, and he was going to hurl the stone across the river, and then run round, over the hump-back bridge, pull the string tight, and cut it at the point where it reached the other bank.

Then he'd run back, over the hump-back bridge, untie the string from the stick and haul it in. Then all he had to do was measure the string – not too difficult.

He fastened the stone to the end of the string.

He threw the stone across the river.

The stone flew through the air beautifully. But it slipped out of the loop he'd made for it at the end of the string. The string fell in the river.

Leslie pulled it out.

He started to cross the hump-back bridge, believing he had

to find the stone he'd already thrown, before it occurred to him that any stone would do.

He hurried back to the stick.

There were lots of stones by the water's edge, but most of them were too small.

Eventually he found a suitable one.

He fastened it to the end of the string.

Again he threw.

Again the wretched stone sailed away, leaving the string dangling in the water.

This time there was an angry shout from near where the stone had landed.

'Get down, men! They're firing! It's a trap! A trap, I tell you! We're all doomed! And me so young!'

Another voice: 'Oh, shut up, Derek. Any stone hit your head, I pity the stone.'

Leslie recognised the second voice as Tilt's.

Heads appeared above the tall nettles and rose bay willow herb – Steve, Wayne, Sharon and Tilt. No sign of Mark or the Great Dalrymple.

Leslie waved. They saw him.

'It's Les,' he heard Sharon say.

The Gang trooped over the bridge.

'Whatcha throwin' stones at Derek for?' said Wayne.

'Does he have to have a reason? I reckon it's a great idea.' Tricia smiled sweetly and stuck her tongue out at Derek.

'I wasn't throwing stones at anyone,' Leslie said, and went on to explain what he had been trying to do.

'We'll help,' said Steve.

'Course we will,' said Derek, rolling up his sleeves. 'Help? I should say so – why, helpin's what we're best at. Known for it – for miles around!'

Tricia tied the string round yet another stone. She walked up to Derek.

'Open your gob,' she ordered.

Derek did as he was told.

Tricia shoved the stone in his mouth.

There was an interesting clonking, grinding sound, a bit like an old cement mixer.

'Aaarrrgghumpff!'

'Good boy,' said Tricia. 'Over the river you go! Run!'

Holding out his hands like the forepaws of a dog, Derek lifted one foot, sniffed the air, and, stone in mouth, string hanging down, slithered down the bank and into the stream.

'Go on, boy! Good boy!' Tricia, giggling, urged him on.

Lifting his feet high, like a little dog crossing a big river, Derek crossed to the other side. He climbed up the far bank to tumultuous applause from the Gang.

He took the stone out of his mouth.

'Can I throw it back at you now?'

'Nitwit! Course you don't. Pull the string tight!'

Derek yanked hard at the string. The stick it was tied to was pulled out of the ground.

'Stop! Stop!'

Steve just managed to grab the stick before it was pulled into the river.

'Derek!' Steve called across to him.

'Yeah?'

'Hold the string tight against the edge of the river bank, and then cut it.'

'The river bank?'

'The string. Cut the string.'

'What with?'

'Marvellous. It'll be Christmas before we get this done,' said Tricia.

Tilt had crossed the bridge.

'Come 'ere with that string,' she said to Derek.

In her hand she had a knife.

It reminded Leslie, for an instant, that these were 'rough' children. The sort that carried knives around.

''Old the string tight, with yer 'ands apart.' Tricia was telling Derek what to do.

'You're not goin' to arrest me?' said Derek. 'No, please, not that, anything but that! I swear I never meant no 'arm, 's God's truth. I was puttin' that money back *into* the safe. Oh, guvnor, think of me family. Me white 'aired mother.'

'Shut up a minute, an' 'old the blessed string tight.'

Derek did as he was told, as he always did.

Tilt cut through the string.

Derek smiled: ''S easy when you know how, innit?' he said.

Tilt ran back over the bridge to join the rest of the Gang.

Steve pulled the string across. He handed it to Leslie.

'There you are,' he said. 'Now you can work out how wide the river is, but why do you want to know?'

If he told them the truth, they'd laugh.

'You don't *have* to tell us,' said Steve.

There was something in the way Steve said that, that made Leslie's eyes go very hot and stingy. What was worse, he sensed the others noticed.

He still had more than a slight fear that they would laugh. He swallowed hard. He told them.

They were impressed.

They liked the idea.

Leslie repeated what Mrs Hammond had said.

'She's right,' said Derek. 'All a question of speed. 'Ow fast d'you reckon you can pedal? 'Undred miles an hour?'

'It's also a question of the angle of take-off,' said Steve. 'We need the Great Dalrymple for this.'

''S gonna depend 'ow 'eavy 'is bike is,' said Sharon.

'An' 'ow 'eavy 'e is,' said Tricia.

'I know that,' said Leslie. 'I'm thirty two and a half kilos.'

'Strip down.'

What did Tilt mean? Did she want him to try to leap the river without any clothes on?

'Take the mudguards off. Brakes off. Chain guard – the lot.'

Oh, she meant the *bike*!

'Have to choose the right spot.' Steve was looking up and down the river. 'This bit isn't right. Got to be somewhere where you can get a good run at it, Les.'

They spent the next hour making plans. They selected a site, where the river was narrow and the banks clear of shrubs and nettle clumps, and where the banks were also not too high.

Steve, Tricia and Tilt had their doubts about Leslie's ability to leap across safely.

'Soft landin', though, innit?' said Sharon.

'Not with a bike underneath 'im, dimmo,' said Tricia.

Wayne and Derek were more concerned with publicity. They saw this as a good chance to earn fame and possibly fortune.

'You want a good crowd watchin', like Evil Knievel 'ad.'

''Ere, what you want to do – tell all yer mates from school!'

Leslie looked at the ground.

'Haven't really got any mates.'

Derek threw himself down and began to writhe on the ground. 'Alone! All alone! Alone in this big cruel 'eartless world!'

'Shut up, Derek! You ain't got no mates, neither.'

Derek smiled up at them all. 'No, I ain't,' he said. 'You're right.'

'What you want,' said Wayne, 'is posters. Stick 'em all over the place. By the Park Gates. Round the shops. Bus stops. Pubs.'

'An' stickers on all the car windscreens, so's the drivers can't see where they're goin' and 'ave terrible accidents,' said Derek.

'Who's gonna do all these posters, then?' said Tilt.

The problem of publicity was solved, eventually, by the Great Dalrymple.

'It's like at elections. They go round, the candidates, don't they, with loudspeakers on their cars, shouting out about meetings and who people have got to vote for. We can do the same thing on our bikes. Night before. And then again on the morning of Leslie's Leap. Should get a good crowd.'

Chapter 12

The date for Leslie's Leap was fixed for next Saturday. Twelve o'clock. Midday.

He didn't tell Mum and Dad. He hardly spoke to Mum and Dad in the week before his Leap. He was only at home for meals and to sleep at night. He had to be reminded to feed Lennie and Luke, to brush his teeth, to wash, to put warm clothes on if it was a cool day, and cool clothes if it was a hot day. There was a lot of nagging, a lot of moaning and groaning.

But it didn't seem as important as it would have done a few days earlier.

Leslie was so busy.

On Wednesday they had a rehearsal.

He met the Gang by the river, and they marked out his approach run.

'You start here,' said Steve, 'and you pedal as fast as you can to where Tilt's standing, on the river bank. When you reach her you should be going flat out. And that's where you take off, and you aim to land by Derek.'

Derek waved from the opposite bank.

'Head for me, Les,' he called cheerfully, 'and I'll catch you.'

'Now, when you reach the other bank, don't put your brakes on,' continued Steve, ''cos you won't have any once we've stripped your bike right down. You just let your bike run on till you come to a stop.'

The river looked incredibly wide.

'Let's have a practice.' It was Sharon's suggestion.

It was all very well, Leslie thought, 'her' saying 'let's have a practice'. It wasn't 'them' that was going to have the practice. It was him!

'Right,' said Steve. 'In position!'

They spread out. Mark and Wayne were at the start, ready to give Leslie a good shove off. Steve, Tilt and Sharon were at the take-off point on one side of the river. Tilt and Derek were at the hoped-for, aimed-for, longed-for (as far as Leslie was concerned) landing point on the other side of the river.

The Great Dalrymple was standing a little separate from the rest, in a position from which he could have a broad, overall view of what was happening.

'Come on, Les,' said Wayne. 'Over 'ere to the start.'

At tortoise pace, Leslie wheeled his bicycle to the start.

Supposing it all went dreadfully wrong?

Crash! Bang! Wallop!

Into the stream he'd go.

Awful!

They'd all be looking and they'd all laugh – that Derek especially.

Derek chose that moment to call out:

'It's only a practice go, Les. So don't worry if you fall in the river and break your neck.'

He heard the smack Tricia gave Derek for being stupid, and the cry of pretend pain from Derek that followed immediately.

'Come on,' said Sharon. 'We ain't got all day.'

Leslie reached the start.

'Rub the backs of your legs,' called out the Great Dalrymple.

'Why?'

'Tone up your muscles. You must be in tip top condition.'

Very gently, Leslie began to stroke the backs of his legs, or rather, the jeans that covered them.

'No, no, no. Wayne, you rub his legs for him. Only do it really hard!'

Wayne and Mark began ferociously rubbing Leslie's legs.

Ow, ow, ow, ow!

That didn't half bloomin' hurt.

Tears sprang to his eyes.

Please, couldn't he go back to his hutch?

His *hutch*? What was he thinking about?

Be a lion, Leslie – not a guinea pig.

'That's enough.'

Wayne and Mark stopped at the Great Dalrymple's call.

They helped Leslie on to his bike. His legs were now wobbling uncontrollably.

They stood, one on each side of him, supporting him.

Derek gleefully began the count down.

'Looking good,' he said. 'You are cleared for take-off on Runway Six Zero. Into the last few seconds . . . and . . . ten . . . nine . . . eight . . .'

Leslie decided he wanted to go to the lavatory. Now. At once. No argument.

But he couldn't say anything. He opened his mouth, but only a wheezing sort of moan came out.

'. . . four . . . three . . . two . . .'

Should he shut his eyes, or keep them open? No time to decide. No time for anything.

'. . . one . . . zero . . . and we have lift off!'

Indeed they did, or at any rate, they had pedal off.

Thrown forward by Wayne and Mark, Leslie hurtled forward, legs pumping like pistons, heart fluttering, feeling sick, clutching the handlebars so tight he thought he'd sprain all the muscles in his fingers.

He raised his head slightly. As if rushing towards him he could see Steve, Tilt and Sharon, their faces growing bigger and longer by the second. Tilt was leaning further over than he'd ever seen her, Sharon and Steve's mouths hung open, in what seemed to be horror.

And, at the very edge of the bank, Leslie knew he'd fail. He wouldn't get half way over. It would be just like before.

And then he felt strong hands grab him from either side, and he was lifted out of the saddle. Swaying and gasping in the grip of Steve, Sharon and Tilt, he saw his bicycle, his beloved bicycle, emerge from between his legs, and drop, like a badly made paper aeroplane, into the river.

Although a part of him knew he was safe, another part of him was horrified as he saw his bicycle disappear under the water. For goodness sake, how deep was it here?

On the far bank Derek was leaning over and peering down into the water.

'Ladies and gentlemen, there's been a slight hitch here at Mission Control. It looks like our intrepid cyclonaut is attempting to break the underwater cycling record.'

Steve, Sharon and Tilt relaxed their grip. Mark and Wayne came running up.

'What happened?' said Mark.

''E weren't goin' to make it,' said Sharon. 'So we stopped 'im.'

Steve was already attending to the recovery of the bicycle.

'Give us a hand, Wayne.'

He had rolled up his cords and taken off his shoes and socks.

He waded into the water. Although he was easily the tallest of the Gang, the water came well over his knees. He held one hand out towards the bank.

'Grab my hand.'

Wayne took it. Mark held on to Wayne's waist as he leaned over the bank.

Steve reached out and down into the water.

'Got it. Right – help pull me back.'

As they pulled him, he dragged Leslie's bicycle out of the deeper water, holding on to its rear wheel, and brought it to the bank.

Sharon, Tilt and Mark lifted the bicycle safely out of the water. Wayne helped Steve clamber up the bank.

Leslie stood – miserable and very shaken.

The Great Dalrymple clapped his hands together. The Gang became silent.

'That's good,' he said.

Leslie couldn't see what was good about it.

Nor, apparently, did Sharon.

'Go on, then, Clever! What's good?'

'We now know Les won't be able to get across on that bike *as it is*!'

'So what you gonna do about it? Fix rockets?'

'Got a spanner, Steve?'

'Yeah.'

'Strip the bike.'

Steve produced a spanner and set to work.

They left Leslie with the frame, the pedals, the wheels, the chain, the handlebars, and, after a lot of arguing, the saddle. Derek, Sharon and Tilt were for taking the saddle off: Steve and Tricia for keeping it on.

The Great Dalrymple decided the saddle should stay. 'He's got to have something to land his bum on,' he said.

Leslie was grateful – thankful for small, but important, mercies.

Half an hour later they were ready for Leslie's second practice attempt. A little pile of brake blocks, mudguards and a bicycle pump, together with bell and saddle bag, lay on the grass. Leslie gazed at it sadly, wondering if his bicycle would ever be the same, before trudging back to his position.

Wayne and Mark threw him from the start.

It was like a nightmare action replay.

But this time he realized earlier that it wasn't going to work.

He jammed on the brakes.

What brakes?

There weren't any brakes!

He dug both heels in the ground, jarring his legs, his knees, his hips. The front wheel skidded round – his bicycle came to an abrupt stop.

Leslie fell off.

He lay in the cow parsley, blinking at the blue sky, listening to the 'whirr' of the bicycle wheel close by his left ear. It was vaguely pleasant to realize he was still alive, that it didn't seem as though he'd broken his arm or leg, that all his teeth were still firmly fixed in his mouth. The earth was warm. The cow parsley smelt thick with pollen. The grass seemed to close protectively around him.

He felt he'd like to lie there a long time.

He'd like to be lost in the long grass and have all the others go away.

'Now what's the matter?'

It was Sharon, glaring down at him.

'Nothing.'

Stupid remark, but it was a stupid question. The 'matter' was that it was impossible! That was all – completely impossible!

He stood up and grabbed his bicycle.

'I'm going home,' he said.

The Great Dalrymple had climbed to the top of the bank.

'Ramps,' he said. 'A take-off ramp and a landing ramp.'

'And a gap between,' said Derek, gloatingly. 'A great *big* gap between.'

'Yeah,' said Tricia. 'Like the one between your ears.'

'So, who's gonna make these ramps?'

'All of us. Combined operation.'

'Out of what?'

'Timber,' said the Great Dalrymple. 'Wood.'

Leslie remembered the helicopter. All that wood. That home for insects.

If he told them about it, they'd want to go to his home to get it.

But wasn't that what he wanted?

Friends. Friends to come home. To muck about in the

garden with him. To make lots of noise with him. To be told off by the Park Keeper and banned from the shops. To have old people turn their heads at bus stops to go 'tsk, tsk'.

Well?

So what was he going to do then?

'Meet here tomorrow afternoon. And bring timber, saws, nails, hammers and rope. Come on, Sharon.'

The Gang split up and moved away. Towards the flats. Towards their side of the Park.

Leslie collected his brakes and his bell and his mudguards together, cramming what he could in his pockets, tucking the rest under his arm. And then, all by himself, he wheeled his bicycle home.

Chapter 13

The next three days, it rained. Wholeheartedly, as it so often does in the school summer holidays.

Each afternoon, Leslie went to the river and spent a miserable half hour under the trees.

The Gang didn't appear.

Leslie went home and got told off for getting himself and his clothes wet. Mum and Dad were in a bad mood.

'If it's like this next week . . .'

'It's always like this in Wales.'

Wales?

'Are we going to Wales?' said Leslie.

'Yes, dear. On Saturday.'

Saturday? Blimey!

'We can't . . . I can't . . .'

'All booked. All settled. We'd better start getting all the camping equipment out tonight. Checking it.'

Of course! Checking the camping equipment. That was why they were in such a bad mood.

But Saturday was the day after tomorrow!

He'd have to pretend to be ill.

And then?

If they believed him, they'd take him to the doctor, and, if they didn't – well, they'd drag him off to Wales, wouldn't they?

He could hide. Disappear.

Friday night, tomorrow night, creep out of bed and nip into the Park just before they locked the gates at nine o'clock. Hide in the woods – that big wood, on the other side of the railway, Summerhouse Wood. Take some Pepsi and some chocolate and pickled onions for breakfast, and meet up with the Gang on Saturday morning. Or, better still, hide from the Gang as well.

Oh, yes, Leslie said to himself. Then what? When he re-appeared? Eh? Just say, 'Sorry to have kept you waiting.'

Fine welcome home they'd give him then. Knock his block off more likely.

The more he thought about it, the more he decided there was only one thing he could do. Get to the river early. Saturday morning – really early. As soon as it was light. And do the Leap all by himself. That would be better. And there would be no one to share his shame if he failed.

And no one to share his glory if he succeeded. What about that? No one would see him sail over that river, land with a bump and a bounce, and make a victorious circuit of the Park. No one to cheer? To applaud? To congratulate him? To slap him on the back? Well – you could do without slaps on the back, couldn't you? Not a lot of point in having your back bruised, whatever the reason. Nor in having your ear drums burst with cheering.

So – glory? Or satisfaction?

Make a fool of himself? Or just get wet?

Prove something to the Gang? Or prove something to himself?

And then Leslie remembered how it had all started. Just something private. No one else had been involved. He didn't need anyone else involved. All this talk of preparations and toning up muscles and ramps and strip downs and publicity and crowds and crowds of cheering people. Or more likely *jeering* people. That wasn't him. That was them. That was the Gang. The Great Fat Dalrymple. That silly Derek. That rude Sharon. He didn't need all that. He didn't need any of that.

He had decided.

He would leap the river, or not, as the case may be, on Saturday morning. Early. Before Mum and Dad were up and loading the car to go to Wales.

Chapter 14

Leslie didn't enjoy Wales. He didn't think his Mum and Dad did either. The family always went camping, but Leslie couldn't for the life of him see why. All those rows about which way round to put the tent and which pole went where. All those rows about finding a better, cleaner, quieter, emptier camp site. All those rows about keeping everything in its place. They could have rows like that at home. They often did. It would have been far better to have put the tent up in the Park. They could have gone home for meals and baths and to do the washing up. Everything was so much harder, camping.

And he was worried about what would happen when they did get home. Sooner or later they would discover his bicycle. The smashed-in front wheel. The battered frame. The bent pedal.

Leap the river?

It had been disastrous.

He'd gone into the water like a lump of lead. At that still, quiet, early hour of the morning, he'd made a splash that he had expected would wake the neighbourhood. His pain and disappointment at failure had been matched only by his terror that he'd be caught by the Park Patrol or the Police. He wasn't even supposed to be in the Park at that hour in the morning, let alone be engaged in barmy bicycling.

He'd got into the Park by enlarging the gap in the fence at the bottom of the garden, and pushing his bicycle through.

Then, feeling as though the eyes of the world were upon him, he'd cycled across the playing field side of the Park, over the hump-back bridge, and round to the spot selected by the Gang.

He felt so lonely, so isolated, so desolate without them. He wished Sharon and Derek had been there, to make fun of him. To have a good laugh – it seemed such a friendly thing to do. He wished the Great Dalrymple was there, to make grand and outrageous plans. Steve, quietly organizing things. Tilt, Tricia, Mark, Wayne – all of them.

But it was just him – Leslie. All alone with his little Chopper bicycle.

And it was cold.

Half past six in the morning.

Lots of dew on the ground. He'd noticed, with fear that it would lead to his discovery, that the wheels of his bicycle left a clear trail across the grass. A shaky, nervous-looking wavery pair of black lines, crossing and recrossing, like the handwriting of an earwig.

A grey morning. No promise of fine weather. Hardly any sound. An early morning train in the distance. And a lone dog barking a couple of streets away.

He'd found the spot selected by the Gang for his crossing. He made no proper preparations. No rubbing of the muscles. He'd put on his school clothes, knowing that they wouldn't be wanted again until September – over a month for them to dry out if he failed and landed in the water.

If? *When.*

And 'when' it was. Pedal, pedal, pedal, off the bank and into the water. Much, much worse than he'd expected. The jarring crash as his bicycle hit the river bed, as luck would have it, straight on to one of the bigger stones.

How wet and cold the water was. And how deep, for the river was swollen by the recent heavy and continuous rain.

For some stupid reason, as he lay there, paralysed with misery, he remembered a bit of 'The Wind in the Willows'. The bit when Mole upset the rowing boat and fell in the river. But there was no friendly, re-assuring Water Rat to shove an oar under Leslie's arm and tell him it was all right.

No friendly anybody.

No one.

All alone. In the cold, cold river.

With a wrecked bike.

As he dragged his lurching, wounded bicycle home, through the Park, over the hump-back bridge, across the playing fields and back through the gap in the fence, Leslie hoped he would never again in all his life be so unhappy. He had to get home, to get his wet clothes off, to hide his bicycle. But he did so wish he could just lie down, and scream, like a baby, until somebody *had* to come and look after him.

He managed.

He hid his bicycle in the shed, and his wet clothes under the bed. All that he would deal with, when they got back from Wales.

He dried himself silently on a towel from the bathroom, and put his pyjamas back on. He got into bed, and waited, nursing his bruised left arm, and trembling a little, until Mum called out to him to get up.

Feeling guilty, and frightened, and disappointed, and hurt, and lonely – he went to Wales.

It was no wonder he didn't enjoy it.

They came back a week later, on the following Saturday. They arrived at 143 Parkside Crescent a little after tea time. The journey had been long, and hot, and sweaty, and grumpy. Sometime in the next few days he'd have to face up to the aftermath of his Leap.

The great Leslie's Leap!

He helped his mum and dad unpack the car. He listened carefully to what was said, and did as he was told. If it was the last thing he'd do, he'd build up a bit of good will.

The week in Wales had rubbed in how 'on-his-own' he was. How much he relied on Mum and Dad. How much he needed to grow up.

He had played on the beach – alone. Explored the rock pools, wandered along the sea shore.

Even Dad had noticed how lonely Leslie seemed. The small, solitary figure, wading through the shallows, silhouetted against the western sky as the sun hung low. He had played with Leslie. Beach cricket. Throwing the Frisbee. Hopscotch on the sand.

'You need friends,' he had said.

Mum had agreed. She had been saying that for some time.

They had sat at a table outside the pub. A rare, warm evening in Wales. Mum and Dad both relaxed. Leslie full of lemonade and crisps. For a moment he had been tempted to tell them about his Leap.

He could tell that story jolly well, he thought. It wasn't simply a failure. It was a tragedy. Anyone who heard it would be full of sympathy, would be on his side.

Then Dad had said:

'After all, you haven't done anything stupid since that newspaper business. So maybe you are growing up.'

Leslie had decided to keep his mouth shut.

And there he was, back at home, trying to be good, and wondering what would happen when they saw his grubby clothes and damaged bicycle.

And wondering what they'd say. Would they make him stay in? Forbid him going to the Park?

Probably.

Then what chance would he have to make friends?

The week in Wales had made him brutally aware of how much he needed friends.

That was what mattered!

Never mind about heroics – leaping over blooming rivers. So what! Better to paddle your feet in a puddle with a friend, than swim the Channel by yourself.

A mate!

Someone to muck about with!

The family sat down to a late tea.

Mum – she was all right, was Mum. But she did have a lot to do. Didn't seem to have much time for mucking about. And she didn't appear very keen on mucking about.

And Dad. He had such set ideas about what was enjoyable. And he went on and on about 'time being too precious to waste'. But time was the only thing that it was right to waste – not food, or money, or opportunities. Time. There was so much of it, and lots of it was made for trying things out, experimenting, gambling with, wasting. But not in Dad's eyes.

Leslie sighed.

'Tired?' asked his mum.

'A bit,' he said.

'Never mind,' said his dad. 'I expect you'll sleep late tomorrow. And the next day. And the next.' Dad rubbed his eyes. 'Doubtless, you'll be lying in bed on Monday morning when I set off for work. It's a wonderful time – childhood.'

Yeah. It stretched out ahead.

The great long summer holiday.

And no friends.

There was a knock on the door. Loud. Loud. Long. What his mum would call 'impolite'.

Voices.

'All right, Derek,' a girl's voice. 'You don't 'ave to bash the bloomin' thing off its 'inges.'

'We know you're in there! The place is surrounded!' Derek's voice. 'Come out with your hands above your heads. Or your knees above your elbows. Or your feet behind your ears.'

'Try putting your foot in your mouth.' That was Tricia, to Derek.

Leslie's mum and dad were frowning.

'I hope that's not Gary. Or that other one – Lee.'
'No, no, it's not.'
Mounting excitement.
More knocking.
'Whoever it is, they'll split that door in a moment.' Dad was getting his 'stern' look.
'I'll go,' said Leslie, quickly.
He raced to the front door and opened it.
They were all there. The Gang. Leaning against the wall, pulling bits off Dad's best lavender bush, treading on his salvias, filling the path down to the gate.
'Hallo, Les,' said Steve. 'Where you been? You comin' across the Park?'
Leslie didn't know what to say. It was beautiful, what they were doing. He felt the corners of his mouth twitch, and he didn't know whether they were about to point upwards with laughter, or down with tears. But he did know that if he cried, it would be with happiness.
'What for?' he said, stupidly.
'Dunno,' said Steve. 'We'll think of something. There's lots we can do. Got nearly all the summer holidays to come. The Great Dalrymple's got a little scheme goin' in 'is bonce for organising an underwater Rock Concert.'
'Come on, Les,' called Sharon, from the gate. 'Don't keep your mates waitin'!'
Mates!
'Old Wayne ain't stopped laughin' yet about that story of yours. That one of when you pinched them newspapers. An' Derek's found a beetle 'e don't know the name of. Where's that beetle, Derek?'
'In me pocket.'
'Dimmo! What a place to keep it.'
'No, it ain't. We got this book at school. 'S called "Book of Pocket Insects".'
'Not "Book of Pocket Insects"! – "Pocket Book of Insects", stupid!'
'Leslie! Who is it?'

Mum's voice.

She and Dad mightn't approve.

'It's me mates. My friends,' Leslie called back. Then, to Steve. 'I can't come out now, I'm having me tea. I could come out after tea.'

'OK, Les. We'll see you down the Park.'

'Gonna bring your bike?'

There was a lot of laughter. Pleasant laughter, and Leslie joined in.

'Nutty idea that, wasn't it?' said Steve. 'Good job we all got fed up with it.'

'Leslie!'

'I've got to go.'

'See you, Les.'

The Gang moved off. Leslie shut the door. He hurried back to his tea.

He'd get told off for bolting his food. He'd get into rows because he was bound to be back late. Then there were his wet clothes under the bed, his bag of bicycle bits, and the broken machine. More rows.

But, like Steve said, there was nearly all the summer holiday to come.

Weeks to spend mucking about. Muck*in*' about.

With his mates.

At last.

Three minutes later, as he rushed from the house to join the Gang in the Park, Mum held the front door open for him.

She smiled.

'At last,' she said.